A Planet to Win

A Planet to Win

Why We Need a Green New Deal

KATE ARONOFF,
ALYSSA BATTISTONI,
DANIEL ALDANA COHEN,
and THEA RIOFRANCOS

VERSO
London • New York

First published by Verso 2019
The collection © Verso 2019
The contributions © The contributors 2019
Foreword © Naomi Klein 2019

1 3 5 7 9 10 8 6 4 2

Verso
UK: 6 Meard Street, London W1F 0EG
US: 20 Jay Street, Suite 1010, Brooklyn, NY 11201
versobooks.com

Verso is the imprint of New Left Books

ISBN-13: 978-1-78873-831-6
ISBN-13: 978-1-78873-833-0 (US EBK)
ISBN-13: 978-1-78873-832-3 (UK EBK)

British Library Cataloguing in Publication Data
A catalogue record for this book is available from the British Library

Library of Congress Cataloging-in-Publication Data
A catalog record for this book is available from the Library of Congress

Typeset in Monotype Fournier by Hewer Text UK Ltd, Edinburgh
Printed in the UK by CPI Group (UK) Lrd, Croydon CR0 4YY

There is nowhere to go now but forward. But which way is forward?

Roland Wank, chief architect, Tennessee Valley Authority, 1941

CONTENTS

FOREWORD
by
Naomi Klein

The Green New Deal burst onto the political stage when organizers held a sit-in in the office of House Speaker Nancy Pelosi (D-CA) last fall. She dismissed the idea as a "Green Dream, or whatever," but organizers were unfazed. They shot back that the Green New Deal was indeed a dream, a badly needed one about what organized and focused people are capable of accomplishing in the face of a crisis that threatens the habitability of our home. Given how radically and rapidly our societies need to change if we are to avert full-blown climate catastrophe (and given the prevalence of ecological doom and despair), sharing some big dreams about a future in which we do not descend into climate barbarism seemed like a very good place to start.

The interplay between lofty dreams and earthly victories has always been at the heart of moments of deep progressive transformation. In the United States, the breakthroughs won for workers and their families after the Civil War and during the Great Depression, as well as for civil rights and the environment in the sixties and early seventies, were not just responses to crises, demanded from below. They were also the products of dreams of very different kinds of societies, dreams invariably dismissed as impossible and impractical at the time. What set these moments apart was not the presence of crises (which our history has never lacked), but rather that they were times of rupture when the utopian imagination was unleashed—times when people dared to dream big, out loud, in public, together. For instance, the Gilded Age strikers of the late nineteenth century, enraged by the enormous fortunes being amassed off the backs of repressed laborers, were inspired by the Paris Commune, when the working people of Paris took over the governing of their city for months. They dreamed of a "cooperative commonwealth," a world where work was but one element of a well-balanced life, with plenty of time for leisure, family, and art. In the lead-up to the original New Deal, working-class organizers were versed not only in Marx but also in W.E.B. Du Bois, who had a vision of a pan-working-class movement that could unite the downtrodden to transform an unjust economic system. It was the civil rights movement's transcendent dream—whether articulated in the oratory of Martin Luther King Jr. or in the vision of the Student Nonviolent Coordinating

Committee—that created the space for, and inspired, the grassroots organizing that in turn led to tangible wins. A similar utopian fervor in the late sixties and early seventies—emerging out of the countercultural upheaval, when young people were questioning just about everything—laid the groundwork for feminist, lesbian and gay, and environmental breakthroughs.

By the time the 2008 financial fiasco was unfolding, that utopian imagination had largely atrophied. Moral outrage poured out against the banks and the bailouts and the austerity that was sure to follow. Yet even as rage filled the streets and the squares, generations who had grown up under neoliberalism's vice grip struggled to picture something, anything, other than what they had always known. Science fiction hasn't been much help, either. Almost every vision of the future that we get from best-selling novels and big-budget Hollywood films takes some kind of ecological and social apocalypse for granted. It's almost as if a great many of us have collectively stopped believing that there is a future, let alone that it could be better, in many ways, than the present.

The climate movement has suffered from this imaginative asphyxiation for many decades. The mainstream green movement has been very good at describing the threat we face in harrowing detail. But when it came to telling the truth about the depth of systemic change required to avert the worst outcomes, there has long been a profound a mismatch. Change your lightbulbs, we were told for a decade. Plant a tree when you fly. Turn your lights off for an hour a year. The name of the game was always the same: show people how they can change without changing much of anything at all.

As this urgent and exciting book makes abundantly clear, that era of pseudo change is definitively over. The Green New Deal has a long way to go before it constitutes an actual plan to get to zero emissions while battling rampant economic inequality and systemic racial and gender exclusions. But it starts with those goals and puts a whole lot of big and bold ideas on the table to get us planning, organizing, and dreaming in our communities and workplaces. Many commentators have of course declared that none of this is possible. It's too ambitious. Too much. Too late. But that overlooks the crucial fact that none of this began in 2018. The ground for this moment had been prepared for decades outside the headlines, with models for community-owned and community-controlled renewable energy; with justice-based transitions that make sure no worker is left behind; with a deepening analysis of the intersections between systemic racism, armed conflict, and climate disruption; with improved green technology and breakthroughs in clean public transit; with the thriving fossil fuel divestment movement; with model legislation driven by the climate justice movement that shows how carbon taxes can fight racial and gender exclusion; and much more. What had been missing is only the top-level political power to roll out the best of these models all at once, with the focus and velocity that both science and justice demand. That is the great promise of a comprehensive Green New Deal in the largest economy on earth. As is detailed in the pages to come, the original New Deal was rife with failings and exclusions. But it remains a useful touchstone for showing how every sector of life, from forestry to education to the arts to housing to electrification, can be transformed under the umbrella of a single, society-wide mission. And unlike previous attempts to introduce climate legislation, the Green New Deal has the capacity to mobilize a truly intersectional mass movement behind it—not despite its sweeping ambition, but precisely because of it. As the fossil fuel industry ramps up its attacks, the "serious" center will craft whittled-down countermeasures that preserve only the most narrowly defined of climate policies. The promise of the kind of radical Green New Deal described in this book is in rejecting both, pushing not just for the "rapid, far-reaching and unprecedented changes in all aspects of society" that the Intergovernmental Panel on Climate Change has urged, but for us to treat the climate crisis as an opportunity to build an altogether fairer, more leisurely, and more democratic world on the other end. We have a hell of a lot of work to do. What will sustain us in the difficult years to come is a dream of the future that is not just better than ecological collapse, but a whole lot better than the barbaric ways our system treats human and nonhuman life right now.

INTRODUCTION: BAD WEATHER, GOOD POLITICS

Seizing the Future

The streets of New Orleans are running with saltwater and grime. Mardi Gras beads thrown up by overflowing sewers speckle the muck like shiny soap suds. A Category 4 hurricane—officially named Maggie, informally known as Katrina 2—has smashed through the city's defenses.

On CNN, the president looks grim but satisfied. "We saw this coming and we prepared. But we can do better." A Coastal Protection Plan softened the blow: restored wetlands and porous concrete diverted and absorbed a lot of the floodwaters in New Orleans. But the storm's violence was overwhelming. A well-planned evacuation has saved hundreds of thousands of lives. Electric buses conveyed well-fed, hydrated city residents to temporary retreat camps. The death toll is sixty-five: some residents simply refused to evacuate.

Two days after the flooding subsides, hardy residents and unionized relief workers—many hired through a job guarantee program—are repairing roads, buildings, and power lines. Relief vans deliver reused bus batteries to emergency shelters to bolster damaged emergency microgrids while the larger power system is repaired. The Chinese government has sent a small relief crew with an innovative system for grid repair. They're joined by conservation workers from around the country, trained in disaster relief and accustomed to bussing from one extreme weather hotspot to another.

The disaster has caused a national revolt. In Wyoming's Powder River Basin, activists have chained themselves to bulldozers in the country's last coal pit. Climate justice organizers are decrying slow resiliency investments in Black and Indigenous communities. In cities and towns across the country, militant teachers have joined their students on a new round of climate strikes, angry that the US power sector isn't on track to hit net zero carbon until 2036. It's 2027, and solar panels and wind turbines aren't going up fast enough. The protestors want to try harder to hit the 2030 net zero carbon target set in the heady first 100 days of the Green New Deal, in spring 2021. Polls say the majority of Americans agree.

Looking ahead, coastal, drought-ravaged, and wild-fire-scorched communities around the country are having hard conversations. Is it time to retreat? What would it take to stay? Americans are realizing that large-scale climate migration is both international and domestic. Everyone now recognizes what the climate movement has been saying for years. In the twenty-first century, all politics are climate politics.

If the scenario above is disorienting, it's because we rarely see climate narratives that combine scientific realism with positive political and technological change. Instead, most stories focus on just one trend: the grim projections of climate science, bright reports of promising technologies, or celebrations of gritty activism. But the real world will be a mess of all three. Climate disasters are coming—but we can withstand the coming storms and prevent far worse ones from happening. Whether we arrive at the relatively bright scenario described above will come down to politics—material struggle and bold ideas. If we get it right, we'll withstand the disasters that are too late to prevent and keep worse ones from happening, while improving living conditions for most people at the same time. We call our vision a radical Green New Deal to signal the depth and breadth of the change we need.

The Intergovernmental Panel on Climate Change tells us that we need to roughly halve global carbon emissions by 2030 to have a decent chance at keeping warming below 1.5° Celsius—the limit that scientists and activists agree we should aim for to prevent catastrophe. Getting there just might be doable. We can absolutely keep global heating to 2° Celsius—the maximum level that the world agreed on in the Paris Agreement in 2016—although we're currently not on track to meet it. Halving global emissions, given that billions of people live in countries far poorer than the United States and some economies will decarbonize more slowly, means that the United States needs to zero out emissions as fast as humanly possible. We don't know exactly how fast climate breakdown will happen—how quickly coral reefs die, glaciers melt, seas rise, and storms strengthen. What we do know is that the less heating, the better. The faster we act, the better.

Carbon pollution, moreover, is just the most urgent indicator of a broader ecological crisis: mass extinction, polluted freshwater, widespread contamination from plastics, systemic soil exhaustion, insect Armageddon, ecosystem collapse—the list goes on. All these are threats to the vitality of the living world around us and to countless human lives.

But despite the erudite self-loathing of so much climate writing in the liberal press, the enemy isn't us. Humans aren't tainted by original sin—apples are nutritious and low-carbon, have another. Nor are we doomed to self-destruction. We're creative, complicated beings stuck in a capitalist economic system where a tiny number of people direct most major investments to maximize profits, and they shape government action accordingly. That system externalizes costs onto communities and ecosystems, and prioritizes the gilded retirement of CEOs over the long-term habitability of the planet, and the lives of those on it.

Ultimately, capitalism is incompatible with environmental sustainability. That said, we have just over a decade to cut global carbon emissions in half. We don't imagine ending capitalism quite that quickly. In any case, you don't need to share our overall analysis to read the climate science the same way we do: we need drastic change now. As we'll argue through this book, the most effective way to slash emissions and cope with climate impacts in the next decade is through egalitarian policies that prioritize public goals over corporate profits, and target investments in poor, working class, and racialized communities. Today's champions of a Green New Deal remind us that in the United States in the 1930s and early 1940s, during the New Deal and subsequent war mobilization, the federal government put millions of people to work on socially beneficial projects, directing investment toward public works and astonishingly rapid arms building. The point isn't to repeat the past, but to remember what concerted public action can do.

We know that the scale and speed of change we're proposing can seem overwhelming. More gradual measures might have worked if we had started decades ago. But we didn't. By the time climate science was getting regular press in the late 1980s, market fundamentalism had taken over mainstream politics. The results have been dismal. In the past four decades, the rich have gotten richer, wages have stagnated, the cost of living has climbed, and the prison population has skyrocketed. Half the country is poorer now than it was in 1980, and 90 percent of Americans are now poorer than they were before the 2008 crash.[1] Meanwhile, carbon emissions have risen unabated, while US fossil fuel extraction has experienced a golden age. Worldwide, over half of the carbon pollution ever released was emitted after 1988. So much for the "end of history."

We're now witnessing a deep unraveling of American life, which is especially stark for young people and people of color. It's visible in the form of rising student debt, bankruptcies driven by medical bills, and an ongoing housing crisis punctuated by evictions, foreclosures, and utility shut-offs. And then there are the waves of climate-linked disasters: In 2017, Hurricane Harvey flooded Houston; then Hurricane Maria devastated Puerto Rico, killing 2,975 people. In 2018, the deadliest wildfire in California history tore through the state's northern forests, killing eighty-five people and destroying thousands of homes—just a month after the Intergovernmental Panel on Climate Change warned that climate effects would be worse than anticipated. Far deadlier storms, droughts, and heat waves have ravaged communities across the Global South. The climate crisis is entwined—objectively, and in our everyday lives—with a broader crisis of capitalism. Gradualism won't cut it.

Radical change only happens when millions of people are organizing, striking, and marching, shaping politics

---

1   Facundo Alvaredo et al., *World Inequality Report 2018*, wir2018. wid.world; Lisa Dettling et al., "A Wealthless Recovery? Asset Ownership and the Uneven Recovery from the Great Recession," *FEDS Notes*, federalreserve.gov.

and the economy from below. Tackling the climate crisis will require action from unions, social movements, Indigenous peoples, racial justice groups, and others to take back public power from the elites who've presided over the climate emergency. That's why the Green New Deal must combine climate action with attacks on social inequalities. Only then can we build enough public support and grassroots organizing to break the stranglehold of the status quo, and give people reasons to keep fighting for more. Who will march for green austerity? For all its flaws, the original New Deal excelled in creating a positive feedback loop between public spending on collective goods and mass mobilization, thus overcoming anti-socialist hostility from the business class and political elites. A Green New Deal would likewise have to make climate action viscerally beneficial, turning victories into organizing tools for yet greater political mobilization—and for ongoing liberation. Done right, investments in climate action could facilitate real freedom for everyone, the kind that only economic security for all makes possible.

While climate narratives often look decades into the future, this short book's focus is tighter—the pivotal 2020s. We can't address every topic—food systems and migration are especially big omissions. With limited space, we explore a handful of core climate battlegrounds with fresh eyes. We call for winding down fossil extraction and private utilities, putting both under democratic, public control. We tackle labor, a longtime sticking point for environmental action, arguing for a commitment to guaranteed green jobs and making the case for a larger transformation of work. We connect clean energy to housing, transit, and recreation, arguing for a housing guarantee and dramatically expanded options for leisure. And we show how a radical Green New Deal in the United States can strengthen commitments to egalitarian climate action around the world, starting with solidarity with the communities at the frontlines of the mining for renewable energy inputs.

We know that in this same timeline, Republican intransigence and entrenched antidemocratic mechanisms like the Senate and electoral college are real obstacles. In a best-case scenario, a Democratic nominee supportive of massive climate investment would be elected in late 2020, and we'd see major Green New Deal legislation passed during the first 100 days of the new administration. But even a progressive president would face hostility from courts, corporate-backed legislators, giant corporations, and their own party apparatus. We change that political math not by negotiating in the Beltway, but by building power beyond it—through elections and in the streets. Only mass mobilization will turn out demoralized voters of every color and push a slim Democratic Senate majority to eliminate the filibuster or use budget reconciliation. Only pressure from below can force judges, regulatory agencies, and state and local politicians to go along with a Green New Deal.

~

This book is rooted in our reading of the science and social science on climate change, our hands-on research, and our personal and political biographies. Collectively, we've spent years researching, writing, and undertaking labor and political organizing. Two of us are children of Latin American immigrants; inspired by Latin American social movements, we've lived and worked all over the continent, learning from the achievements and limits of the Left in power.

We've all come to the climate fight by different routes. We all see climate change as a grave threat to human flourishing, a clear indictment of our current political and economic system—and an opportunity to do things differently. For most of our lives, climate politics have felt stuck in a loop of abstract reports telling us the window of opportunity is closing and the apocalypse looming. The Green New Deal is the most ambitious and exciting plan we've ever seen in mainstream politics. We want to help articulate its vision—and flesh out some details.

While US action is urgent, it's not enough. Climate breakdown and capitalism are global. But as US residents, this is the political system we have at least some leverage over. The United States is also the belly of the beast. It remains the world's second-largest carbon emitter, behind China. In per-capita terms, US emissions are over twice as high. And our aggregate historical emissions—over one-fifth of the global total—eclipse every other country's. The United States has been the single greatest obstacle to global climate action for decades, and today, it's poised to increase fossil fuel extraction more than any other country.[2] A Green New Deal that turns US climate politics around would be transformative. If the United States joined (and prodded) Europe and China in prioritizing climate-friendly green investment, more than half the global economy would be invested in climate action. Our chapter on the Green New Deal's global implications focuses on how US-based movements might connect to worker and community struggles elsewhere.

A final caveat: This book is full of "shoulds," and even the occasional "must." Please forgive our enthusiasm. We don't mean to lecture, but to enrich debate with clear arguments for what we might accomplish. We hope that in the best case scenario we'll only be a little bit wrong.

The Road to the Green New Deal

We can start by learning from recent climate policy failures. Many Democratic leaders still simultaneously argue that we should blame the lack of climate action on unwavering Republican climate denial, and that bipartisan compromise is the best hope for getting climate legislation passed. Their track record doesn't inspire much confidence.

---

2   Christopher Alessi, "US Expected to Produce Half of Global Oil and Gas Growth by 2025," *Wall Street Journal*, November 12, 2018.

When Barack Obama entered office in 2009 amid the biggest financial crisis since the Depression, he had incredible power to act. But in the early months of his administration, Obama chose to restore the system that had caused the crisis rather than to change it. We know he bailed out the banks instead of nationalizing them, even as 9.3 million households lost their homes. In this context, Obama's team also nixed the idea of a federally built clean energy grid on the grounds that government shouldn't crowd out private actors. They rejected proposals for federal green banks that would fund low-energy building upgrades, clean energy build-out, and high-voltage transmission wires.[3] Instead of using budget reconciliation maneuvers to push a truly progressive package through the Senate by majority vote, Obama reached across the aisle to get a handful of Republicans to support a compromise stimulus—the 2009 American Recovery and Reinvestment Act (ARRA). Nearly a quarter of the $820 billion stimulus went into tax cuts.

The Obama administration did pour $90 billion into clean energy measures through the stimulus package. It included clean energy research and development, subsidized wind and solar build-out, and allocated billions for high-speed rail (most of which wasn't built). Thanks to Fox News, the bankruptcy of stimulus-funded Solyndra

3   Reed Hundt, *A Crisis Wasted: Barack Obama's Defining Decision* (Rosetta Books 2019).

grew infamous, while few knew that the same stimulus established Tesla with billions of public dollars. ARRA really was good for wind, solar, and batteries. So centrists defend Obama's green stimulus on the grounds that it was better than it gets credit for. What they never consider is that he didn't try to make green investment viscerally popular, by tying his clean industrial policy to a transformative government jobs program and housing rescue.

On the contrary, Obama's team fastidiously avoided anything that smacked of socialism. In the eyes of top advisors like Larry Summers and Timothy Geithner, this precluded nearly all major public interventions into the economy. Recall that in late 2008 and 2009, the federal government and Treasury had poured trillions of public dollars into rescuing Wall Street and real estate, effectively putting the government in charge. Obama chose not to use that power to implement Left populist policies that would have helped millions struggling to survive, building the appetite for more aggressive action. He fired Van Jones, his "green jobs czar," to appease the conservative media mere months after taking office. He declined to directly hire millions of workers to make needed infrastructure repairs and restore ecosystems. (In 1934, FDR temporarily hired four million workers to relieve devastating unemployment.) Instead of directly stemming foreclosures through aggressive government action, Obama implemented convoluted and ineffective programs. And he signed onto the Bush administration's wildly unpopular bank bailout, emphasizing continuity for Wall Street's benefit. He wouldn't even restrict bonuses for bank executives saved by bailouts. As he told financial CEOs in early 2009, "My administration is the only thing between you and the pitchforks." Frankly, he should have put unemployed people to work in a solar-powered pitchfork factory.

As the sociologist Theda Skocpol shows, the administration's striving for elite compromise also helped doom the 2009 Waxman-Markey climate bill. Grassroots green groups were sidelined, while a handful of NGOs and fossil fuel executives haggled behind closed doors, wasting what was left of the precious political opening created by the crisis.[4] Although the bill made major concessions to the fossil fuel industry and other business interests, it still collapsed in the Senate in 2010.[5]

In his second term, Obama accelerated regulations to make the economy more energy efficient and shut down coal plants. He signed the Paris Agreement, a modest achievement hyped as a major victory. The low-carbon pledges made by signatory countries failed to match the Agreement's stated goal of keeping warming below 2° Celsius. The biggest bottleneck in global climate politics remained the United States.

---

4   Theda Skocpol, "Naming the Problem: What It Will Take to Counter Extremism and Engage Americans in the Fight against Global Warming," Harvard University, prepared for the symposium on the politics of America's fight against global warming, 2013, scholars.org.

5   Ryan Lizza, "As the World Burns," *New Yorker*, October 3, 2010.

Fundamentally, the limits of Obama's climate policies reflected the broader failures of the United States center-left's neoliberal turn, premised on the idea that bipartisan consensus could pass reasonable policies to advance the common good—without the common people getting in the way. As historian Adam Tooze observes, "Obama's administration never built the constituency of Democrats-for-life that was shaped by Roosevelt's New Deal."[6] This failure made it all too easy for Trump to win the electoral college by promising to bring manufacturing jobs back to the rust belt, which had never really recovered from the 2008 crash—or, for that matter, from Bill Clinton's North American Free Trade Agreement (NAFTA). Four-and-a-half million Obama voters, half of them people of color, stayed home in November 2016.[7] And now Trump is threatening a climate apocalypse. Can a return to mild progressivism really stem the tide of authoritarian, conservative oligarchy?

Brad DeLong, an economist who helped lead the Democrats' neoliberal era, recently admitted that project's failure: "Over the past 25 years, we failed to attract more Republican coalition partners, we failed to energize our own base, and we failed to produce enough large-scale obvious policy wins to cement the center into a durable governing

---

6   Adam Tooze, *Crashed: How a Decade of Financial Crises Changed the World* (Viking 2018), p. 280.

7   Philip Bump, "4.4 million 2012 Obama voters stayed home in 2016 — more than a third of them black," *Washington Post*, March 12, 2018.

coalition." DeLong's message for his centrist friends? "The baton rightly passes to our colleagues on our left."[8]

Today's young climate activists have seized the baton and turned it into a torch. In that, they're joining the broader wave of movements that have shaken the post-Katrina, post-2008 world, declaring that business as usual must end if we're to have a future.

In late 2018, the charismatic democratic socialist Alexandria Ocasio-Cortez upset a longstanding Democratic congressman in a New York primary, got elected to Congress, and immediately made the Green New Deal a priority. Before she was even sworn in, she joined Sunrise Movement protesters sitting in at Nancy Pelosi's office. A month later, Ocasio-Cortez and climate stalwart Senator Ed Markey (D-MA) released a resolution calling for a Green New Deal.[9]

The resolution calls for massive public investment to get the US economy to net zero carbon in the 2030s (the exact timeline is ambiguous). Connecting the climate crisis to economic misery, it calls for a job guarantee, wherein the public sector would provide a job to any US resident who wants one. The resolution also echoes legislation in California and New York State by prioritizing clean energy and resiliency investments in racialized and working-class

8   Zach Beauchamp, "A Clinton-era Centrist Democrat Explains Why It's Time to Give Democratic Socialists a Chance," *Vox*, March 4, 2019.

9   Danielle Kurtzeblen, "Rep. Alexandria Ocasio-Cortez Releases Green New Deal Outline," *NPR*, February 7, 2019.

communities, and it calls for expanding and improving access to a huge range of social services through programs like free public college tuition and Medicare for All. Other issues, like housing and agriculture, are mentioned in passing. Environmental and climate justice movements, progressive greens, and some major labor unions have organized around these ideas for decades. Their arguments were finally reflected in a high-profile national policy framework.

The AOC-Markey climate program marks a radical break from the Obama era of climate policy, which sometimes used the language of the Green New Deal but failed to live up to the rhetoric. The Green New Deal resolution, by contrast, offers a program of economic transformation that shouts its ambition from the rooftops. Its realism isn't grounded in Beltway savvy but the world's best climate science. Its vision is on the scale of an existential threat to human civilization. But it's also short on concrete next steps.

The battle over the Green New Deal's meaning has begun, with pundits, grassroots movements, and presidential aspirants staking out clearer and more prominent positions on climate change than ever before. Many centrist economists, wonks, and pundits have tried to ride the new wave of excitement around climate policy, using the language of the Green New Deal to describe programs with far less ambition.[10] We call their alternative the "faux Green New Deal."

---

10   For example, see Editorial Board, "Want a Green New Deal? Here's a Better One," *Washington Post*, February 4, 2019.

In the view of these cautious moderates, decarbonizing the economy by the mid 2030s—or even just the energy sector!—is absurdly ambitious. Faux Green New Deal advocates see the plan's social agenda as an expensive distraction. They believe that carbon taxes, with refunds for the poor, and heavy investments in research and development (R&D), should be the main policies that decarbonize the economy—gradually, but efficiently. To be fair, it's a coherent approach. Their view is that climate progress is most likely to happen if it's simple and narrow in scope—focused mainly on energy, minimally intrusive in everyday life, and garnering agreement among policy elites. For these skeptics, it's precisely because inequalities are so entrenched that it would be reckless to hinge decarbonization on struggles for universal, quality social services and public control over markets. Getting to net zero carbon in the United States in ten years—or even twenty—will be hard enough. Why add the extra burdens of dismantling inequalities and disciplining capital? Why not save the world today, then make it better tomorrow?

The Practical Case for Radicalism

The real "green dream, or whatever," to borrow a phrase from Nancy Pelosi, is that the "faux Green New Deal" will work.[11] One simple argument structures this book:

---

11 "Pelosi calls the Green New Deal 'the green dream or whatever,'" *The Week*, February 7, 2019.

An *effective* Green New Deal is also a *radical* Green New Deal.

When we talk about a radical Green New Deal, we don't mean a fringe position. Our word radical comes from the Latin *radix*, meaning root: radical change is systemic change that tackles root causes rather than merely addressing symptoms. Is that too much to fight for in the United States? We agree with Ocasio-Cortez's statement on *60 Minutes:* "It only has ever been radicals that have changed this country."[12] We think a radical Green New Deal would also be a popular one. We aim to build a climate politics for the 99 percent: the multiracial masses against a tiny elite, demanding justice for all on a livable planet.

More concretely, what does it mean to get at the roots of climate change?

For one thing, we're taking the science seriously and setting our political goals accordingly. The faux Green New Deal logic of gentler targets and slower change effectively accepts global heating of 3° Celsius, risking even more if climatic feedbacks kick in fast. Our goal is a *maximum* of 2° Celcius of warming, aiming for as close to 1.5° Celsius as we can get. What's more, while the faux Green New Deal uses tax incentives and price signals as its economic levers, the radical Green New Deal would use the power of public investment and coordination to prioritize decarbonization at speed, scope, and scale. And while

---

12   *60 Minutes*, CBS News, June 23, 2019.

the faux Green New Deal focuses narrowly on swapping clean energy for fossil fuels, we see energy as connected to broader physical systems and social inequalities. A radical Green New Deal leans in to the inevitable intersections of social, economic, and environmental policy, and prioritizes equality.

Finally, the faux Green New Deal sees the scope and ambition of a radical Green New Deal as a political liability. The faux Green New Deal seeks to achieve change by maximizing elite consensus and making policy under the radar. In contrast, we see the broadening of climate policy as a political asset: it's an opportunity to build majority support for big change and mobilize political energies to break the status quo. Let us explain in more depth.

We start with our core priority: avoiding climate collapse. We don't know exactly how sensitive the climate system is. Planning for 2.5° or 3° Celsius of warming, as the faux Green New Deal's gradualism implicitly does, accepts devastating impacts in Global South countries and risks an apocalyptic 4.5° Celsius. So we're shooting for 1.5° Celsius. We'd rather miss an all-out 2030 power sector decarbonization plan by a few years than miss a slower, easier 2040 target, where failure would have graver consequences. As bad as US weather is getting, in the near term African and Asian countries will bear the greatest brunt of 3° Celsius warming. We're not willing to let that happen just to make life easier for ExxonMobil and Wall Street.

And we're more worried about the carbon budget than the fiscal deficit. Our bottom line is the scientific consensus that the 2020s will require, as a recent essay in *Science* put it, "Herculean" efforts to transform the economy.[13]

Herculean change isn't the specialty of market nudges. To decarbonize fast, we have to take democratic, public control of much of the economy to put equitable climate action first. Remember: Capitalists invest in projects to make money and consolidate their power, not to make the world a better place. If the latter happens, it's a happy side effect. Even if some corporate executives worry about the world that awaits their grandchildren, they will never sacrifice profits to cut carbon emissions. If they did, their shareholders would replace them.

The faux Green New Deal tries to harness capitalist investment for climate benefit mainly through R&D funding, mild subsidies, and pricing carbon. They see a carbon tax as the main engine driving the private sector toward lower carbon investments, incentivizing companies and consumers alike to decarbonize. They also want to prioritize R&D for new technologies like large-scale geothermal energy, alternatives to conventional meat protein, and direct air capture of carbon. We agree on ramping up R&D. It's just no substitute for dramatically accelerating deployment of the excellent clean technology we already have.

---

13   Johan Rockström et al., "A Roadmap for Rapid Decarbonization," *Science*, vol. 355, no. 6331, March 24, 2017.

We also support a progressive carbon tax, with a rebate for low- and middle-income people. A modest price on carbon can help knock out coal, which is already on the ropes. If well-designed, it can help steer people away from carbon-intensive consumption, encouraging us to spend our extra cash on dance classes instead of a new iPad, and can help government agencies and firms plan long-term investments to account for climate change. But pricing carbon is a secondary tool, a complement to our principal levers of public spending, coordination, and regulation, all aimed at raising the general standard of living. Without accessible no-carbon alternatives, jacking up the price of gas will just cause a huge political backlash. Carbon pricing is also an oddly indirect strategy for rapid change. As the journalist David Roberts joked during a 2018 lecture in Philadelphia, the United States didn't defeat the Nazis by taxing factories that didn't produce planes and tanks for the war effort.

For the United States to get to net zero emissions in its power sector by the mid-2030s, the country needs to build out new clean energy at least ten times faster than in recent years. Along with public investments in ecosystem restoration, green infrastructure, and conservation work, these measures would require an enormous amount of labor— and thus create millions of high-quality green jobs. There's simply no precedent for the private sector mobilizing that broadly and quickly. With state support, green capitalists have developed cheap and effective clean energy technologies. But while solar companies can gradually outcompete coal, they can't legislate coal out of existence or transform the electricity grid and broader energy system.

Under a radical Green New Deal, the public sector would direct investment and coordinate production, much as it did during World War II. Can government bureaucracies handle such complex work? They could seventy-five years ago, working with legal pads and chalkboards. In the 1940s, improvised public agencies, the army, and government-subsidized businesses ramped up the production of killing machinery with unbelievable speed. The public-backed industry built the world's largest factory in under a year near Ypsilanti, Michigan; it went on to produce a B-24 bomber every hour. Overnight, car seat factories switched to parachute production and Cadillac assembly lines started churning out tanks.[14]

We wish we had a different analogy for that scale of public action than World War II. But the point remains: we can build—and push—a public sector capable of stewarding a rapid and just transition. It's often forgotten, moreover, that state capacity was built up in the decade prior by the New Deal. Neoliberals have spent four decades chipping away at these administrative capacities, weakening

---

14   Bill McKibben, "A World at War," *New Republic*, August 15, 2016. Also see Mark R. Wilson, *Destructive Creation: American Business and the Winning of World War II* (University of Pennsylvania Press 2016).

regulations and many federal agencies to empower big business. Rebuilding and reinvigorating public institutions is one of the most important tasks we face today.

Much of what we're proposing is called industrial policy. It's widespread in Europe, East and Southeast Asia, and beyond; it featured in ARRA's success stories. More broadly, in the United States, state-funded military research has spawned most of the technologies at work in smartphones—like GPS, the internet, and microprocessors. The National Institute of Health and the Department of Energy's Advanced Research Projects Agency-Energy (ARPA-E) program regularly fund pathbreaking innovations. Most infrastructure development already combines public and private investment. Big states like California and New York are already experimenting with Green New Deal tools like aggressive regulations, green banks, and targeting green investments in marginalized communities.

Popular participation will be essential to make sure a large-scale mobilization doesn't run roughshod over people's lives. Federal power doesn't have to mean top–down control. Labor unions, nonprofits, and community groups should all help steer the transition. As in Germany, we could foster energy community cooperatives for solar and onshore wind. In working class communities, which are disproportionately Black and brown, investment could empower people to make decisions over production and direct funds toward their needs. All this could help orient the state away from mass incarceration and toward community welfare.

We would also expand nonmarket institutions that are accountable to and run by communities, not governments—like public credit unions and utilities, land trusts, and worker cooperatives. And we would welcome worker co-ownership of large private companies, through arrangements like the "inclusive ownership funds" being debated in the United States and United Kingdom. Federally funded projects would be locally controlled. Picture libraries doubling as resiliency centers, community gardens employing neighborhood residents, and cooperatives of contractors weatherizing homes. The point isn't to give Washington, DC, more power for centralization's sake, but for federal spending to empower communities at various scales to better control their own lives.

Ultimately, the carbon-tax-first approach of faux Green New Deal boosters posits microeconomics as the solution to the climate crisis, when what we really need is a new political economy. Averting catastrophe means transforming consumption and production, prioritizing shared public goods that improve overall quality of life over the consumption of cheap, carbon-rich crap that we don't need. We should all eat less meat and fly for fun less often. But we have to change collectively—and for that, we need no-carbon alternatives. Public agencies would drive the big change, providing green jobs in place of environmentally destructive work; building guaranteed public housing, parks, and playgrounds; and expanding no-carbon services like free health care and education. As we explain throughout the book, investing in equality isn't just a feel-good add-on: it's our most effective and efficient lever for decarbonizing, by making the good life compatible with lower resource use.

It's the rich who will bear the brunt of climate sacrifice. They've reaped almost all the benefits of economic growth for decades, and they've spent it lavishly. Globally, the wealthiest 10 percent are responsible for half the world's carbon footprint.[15] In the United States, the richest tenth of the population is responsible for a quarter of emissions.[16] Cutting their consumption would have a far greater ecological impact than anything the rest of us can do individually. Climate scientist Kevin Anderson estimates that if the wealthiest 10 percent of people worldwide consumed at the level of the average European, global carbon emissions would drop by roughly a third.[17] The wealthy also funnel the billions they don't consume into investments that diminish our common world—from uninhabited luxury apartments in New York and San Francisco to

---

15 Oxfam International, "Extreme Carbon Inequality," December 2, 2015, oxfam.org.

16 Kevin Ummel, "Who Pollutes? A Household-Level Database of America's Greenhouse Gas Footprint," Center for Global Development, Working Paper 381, October 10, 2014, cgdev.org.

17 Kevin Anderson, "Response to the IPCC 1.5°C Special Report," *Manchester Policy Blogs*, October 8, 2018, blog.policy.manchester.ac.uk.

venture capital thrown at rideshare companies displacing public transit.

To reuse, recycle, and—most importantly—redistribute on a massive scale, a radical Green New Deal would levy higher wealth, inheritance, and upper-level income taxes to slash luxury consumption and help fund public luxuries.

Such a monumental project will take a lot of what's often referred to as "political will," or what we prefer to call political *power*. This is where the difference between our vision and that of the faux Green New Deal comes to a head. Green policy elites often assume that change comes from above: if only some politicians were bold enough to lead on climate action, the people would follow. We think it works the other way around.

Elitist narratives about climate change often suggest that ordinary people can't understand it and will never sacrifice for the benefit of future generations or distant others. But we think the real problem is that ordinary people have been stripped of their power. Starting in the 1970s, the US business class has crushed labor unions— one of our greatest vehicles for equality. The percentage of workers represented by unions has been halved; in that same time, workers' real wages stagnated, even as their productivity increased. The share of income going to the top 10 percent of earners nearly doubled, and the 1 percent did even better. This wasn't only an economic change—it was also a political one. The super-rich seized even greater control of political parties, rewriting laws at every level of government for their own benefit.

As the country's elite dismantled both unions and public power, they also strengthened big business and the fossil fuel sector. Leading capitalist associations—the Business Roundtable, the US Chamber of Commerce, the National Association of Manufacturers, and so on—have helped hand Big Oil tax breaks and regulatory rollbacks. The Democrats helped too.

To break the power of the reigning elite and impose public priorities on the economy, we need to build a mass coalition of ordinary people. Rebuilding public power will require tackling the inequalities and divisions that capitalism sows, both among US working families and across borders. Things are now so bad that most Americans are ready for change, as recent political turmoil makes clear. A radical Green New Deal doesn't try to side-step all this political energy—it builds on it for the common good.

Beyond Bad Dichotomies

We see public investment and popular mobilization as non-negotiable elements of the radical Green New Deal. Yet prospects for climate action tend to rouse sharp debate around old dichotomies, especially on the Left. Polemicists charge that you're either a cornucopian or a Malthusian, an eco-modernist or a Luddite. We think drawing strict, abstract lines on science, technology, and particular economic tools can distract us from more fundamental questions. Instead of fetishizing or demonizing technologies, we call for evaluating them the way we would any other political project: Do they reduce the amount of carbon in the atmosphere and advance human freedom? Who controls them, and for what purposes?

Capitalism likes to tout technology as a wonder drug—let corporations charge enough for their products and they'll solve all our problems. We know technology won't "solve" climate change while leaving the rest of the world intact. But we also shouldn't let the military or Silicon Valley own or define "tech"—literally or metaphorically. Science and technology can help us understand, and live with, the planet we share.

We're skeptical that there will be viable technologies to capture and store carbon burned by natural gas plants on an industrial scale or to produce limitless quantities of clean energy with no social or ecological cost. But if someone developed cold fusion or a giant decarbonizing machine tomorrow, we'd be thrilled—as long as ExxonMobil didn't hold the patent. We want to keep open every nuclear plant that can run safely until we reach net zero carbon and can replace nuclear energy with solar and wind.

In short, we see no reason to arbitrarily decide in advance which technologies will ultimately be sustainable or morally preferable. We want the longest possible list of options for quickly slashing carbon. We want to build power for better technology, inspired by calls for a new digital commons that would put the power of machine learning and algorithms under transparent, democratic control. And we want to radically loosen patents to speed global cooperation on clean tech, making the best tools available to all countries. The possibility of technological miracles in the future can't be an excuse to do less now. As we've argued, we want to increase public research and development *and* accelerate deployment of no-carbon technologies we already have.

This book also doesn't parse debates around how to pay for a radical Green New Deal. You may or may not accept the tenets of modern monetary theory, which holds that the government can produce almost unlimited money for useful investment. Either way, there's broad economic agreement among a range of progressive schools of economic thought that the conditions are favorable for at least a few years of massive, public green investment. We've had decades of low interest rates; there's fiscal room for maneuver; the Fed has a panoply of tools to prevent runaway inflation; green bonds are an exploding market that we could tap. There are also countless reasons to increase taxes on the wealthy, which can help fund social benefits, clean energy deployment, and research and development. There are hundreds of billions to be redirected from the military and fossil fuel subsidies. Meanwhile, the future costs of unabated climate change are incalculable. In the last three years, the average cost of climate-related disasters in the United States alone was $150 billion per year. We know that we have enough money and economic consensus to start funding a radical Green New Deal now—and that we can't afford not to.

Even if a magic decarbonator miraculously appeared overnight, we'd still have an ecological crisis. This raises the most contentious dichotomy of all: growth or degrowth. GDP growth has never been a great metric for the things we care about. The past forty years show that it can continue without benefiting most people's well-being or trickling down. Contrary to the ideology of capitalism, materially intensive growth can't continue forever. We can't pretend ecological limits don't exist. And contrary to the arguments of clean technophiles, there's zero evidence that growth can be meaningfully "decoupled" from resource use, or occur without environmental impact. Our view is that we need a "Last Stimulus" of green economic development in the short term to build landscapes of public affluence, develop new political-economic models, jump off the growth treadmill, break with capital, and settle into a slower groove.

Reconnecting the Dots

The old ecological adage is right: everything is connected. The planet and its atmosphere are the material base on which all other human activity rests. Today, capitalism drives most of that activity. At every turn, carbon emissions are entangled with the drive for profit and filtered through the lived realities of race, class, gender, and place.

Yet policy discussions tend to divide climate change into silos, offering analyses sector by sector—buildings, transportation, power plants, agriculture—and targeted solutions for addressing them one at a time. But each issue intersects with others in countless ways. Climate change, the economy, social inequalities—they're all tied up together. So we break the problem down in a way that emphasizes the connections between politics, economics, and carbon, using a holistic, political economy approach that could be applied to any number of issues.

A Planet to Win devotes a chapter each to four strategic battlegrounds: fossil fuels and private utilities; labor; the built environment; and the global supply chains of a renewable transition. In each, we explore our vision of what a Green New Deal could do and how to dig into the struggles ahead.

For a stable climate and a more equal world, we have to simultaneously unmake our fossil-fueled lifestyles and build infrastructures that equitably distribute renewable energy. We have to dismantle the most powerful industry on earth incredibly fast, or the things we build to replace it won't matter. That means tackling fossil capital head on.

To do that, we'll need the power that comes with a renewed labor movement—which means overcoming long-standing tensions between labor and environmental politics. There's a lot of work to do to build a world that runs on sunshine. But all the work we'll need to retrofit homes and erect wind turbines, solar arrays, and transmission lines doesn't exhaust the category of "green jobs." Far from it. In our vision, care work—construed broadly to encompass reproducing our communities and restoring the planet's ecosystems—is just as essential to a green economy.

Even the energy transition itself isn't just about swapping out one energy source for another. Energy systems are embedded in everyday life: they shape everything from transit to housing to the landscapes traversed by power lines. We dig into the guts of all these systems to show how at every turn, remaking our built environment is wrapped up with politics—and opportunities for liberation.

Finally, we have to track the implications of an energy transition beyond US borders. A transition in the United States can't come at the cost of more devastation elsewhere. Basic solidarity means respecting the democratic will of communities who supply the lithium, cobalt, copper, and other resources needed to produce renewable energy and who bear the brunt of extraction's effects. Building solidarity across borders is the best way to strengthen global climate cooperation rooted in justice.

Coda: The Next Crisis

At the time of writing, in summer 2019, the Trumpian nightmare feels ghoulishly routine. But change comes in volcanic bursts, and the magma beneath us is boiling. Over the last two centuries, organized movements have repeatedly built enough strength to make vast social change, transforming worldviews and material conditions: the abolitionists of the nineteenth century, the movement for women's suffrage, the radical labor movement, the civil rights movement, queer liberation. Broad majorities for radical change always start as militant minorities. Today, militant organizing is everywhere, from the explosive growth of the Democratic Socialists of America to the teachers' strike wave to the migrants' rights movement, and increased mobilization around racial justice, housing justice, reproductive justice, and Indigenous rights. Even scientists are marching on Washington.

There's also the matter of crisis. President Obama wasted his, but more are on the horizon. A global economic slump looms; climate disasters are unfolding faster than ever. Ecological and economic crises are sure to coincide and mutually reinforce. At the time of writing, Americans are struggling to make their car loan payments, and student debt is obliterating the bank accounts of millions of millennials. There are billions of dollars in real estate value in housing markets that are literally about to go underwater—forever—in places like Miami Beach. Oil majors, some of the world's biggest companies, are valued based on their reserves—which contain roughly five times as much carbon as we can burn without destroying civilization. The Bank of England is warning all who will listen about these "stranded assets." In 2008, we saw what a few million bad mortgages could do to a hyperfinancialized, overleveraged, and interconnected global economy. Worse is coming.

We don't celebrate or romanticize brutal breakdowns of social, economic, and political stability. But as Naomi Klein showed to such devastating effect in her book *The Shock Doctrine*, the Right plans for crises meticulously. We should, too. If we can organize in advance, we can use the openings created by the next crises to directly attack their root causes. No more crises wasted.

Whenever they strike, those coming crises will be chances to charge forward with our organizing. And when market crashes coincide with progressives and leftists holding state power, militant organizing proliferating, and millions marching in the streets, our leverage will be huge. Each win that cuts carbon and betters everyday life lays the groundwork for more. The premise of a radical Green New Deal is that we're entering a new era for politics—a whole new terrain, material and imaginative, for deciding how to channel our collective energies. The future is coming at us fast—but we still have the chance to shape it. We have nothing to lose, and a planet to win.

1

BURY THE FOSSILS

Aluminum has a melting point of 1,220° Fahrenheit. If you aren't a welder or a chemist, there's no practical reason to know this. From beer kegs to the foil we wrap our leftovers in, aluminum is ubiquitous. But it's one of the less charismatic elements on the periodic table, not a show-off like neon or cobalt or a celebrity like carbon.

More carbon in the atmosphere has helped make ten of the last fifteen years the hottest on record. Fourteen of the largest twenty wildfires in California history have occurred over the same period: less rain and higher temperatures create petri dishes for wildfires to spark. Climate change increases the variability in rain and temperature, and a wet winter one year can sprout vegetation that becomes kindling during a dry season the next. The Camp Fire, which leveled the town of Paradise, killed eighty-six people after sparks from a poorly maintained transmission line owned by mammoth California power provider PG&E met the surrounding brush.

Those trying to escape flames were surprised as their cars' aluminum rims turned molten, splaying out onto the overheated pavement. Drivers who managed to flee on foot found that their shoes melted to the road as they ran. Rubber melts at 356° Fahrenheit. Many didn't make it out. Flames burned so hot, one local official in Alameda County told the *New York Times*, that there was no DNA left on human remains; emergency response officials and cadaver dogs sorting through the ruins often found only unidentifiable bone fragments. "People have been cremated, for lack of a better term," he said.[1]

Breaking the Chain

It's rare to be able to name who caused climate impacts with confidence. We can't blame any given weather event on a coal or oil company any more than we can pin a particular lung cancer death on a particular cigarette company, however often the deceased lit up Marlboro Reds. Yet just ninety greenhouse-gas-producing companies—almost all privately held or state-owned fossil fuel producers—have been responsible for two-thirds of planet-warming emissions since the dawn of the industrial age; half of those

---

1   Thomas Fuller and Richard Pérez-Peña, "In California, Fires So Fast Hesitation Proved Lethal," *New York Times*, October 13, 2017.

were released in the last thirty years.[2] As state investigators in California found, a private utility squeezing out extra profits by neglecting maintenance of its power lines is responsible for the sparks igniting them. From extraction to delivery to lobbying, the fossil fuel industry and private utilities work hand-in-hand as the masters of an energy system dominated by shareholders and driven by all the wrong priorities.

To keep warming below 2° Celsius, about four-fifths of known fossil fuel reserves must *not* be dug up and burned. And yet companies' valuation is premised on the expectation that everything they own will be sold and combusted. The fossil fuel industry's business model, and hence their executives' prerogative, is to grow their reserves and burn every last drop. The industry's ongoing existence is thus incompatible with the future of anything we might recognize as human civilization. The Green New Deal should dismantle our profit-driven energy system just as aggressively as it constructs a clean energy alternative. It's the only way to stop the carbon pollution that's driving the climate emergency and to crush the companies erecting the greatest political obstacles to decarbonizing.

It's easy to forget how simple this problem is when we navigate our own little energy landscapes. We can flick a

---

2   Richard Heede, "Tracing Anthropogenic Carbon Dioxide and Methane Emissions to Fossil Fuel and Cement Producers, 1854–2010," *Climactic Change* 122: 1–2 (2014), pp. 229–41.

switch without much thought for the long-dead creatures compacted into coal, oil, and gas, their unrecognizable carcasses exhumed by fossil fuel companies and shipped around the world to be incinerated, unleashing heat-trapping greenhouse gasses into the atmosphere and threatening millions now living. Left unchecked, the death toll of climate change could easily creep up into the hundreds of millions—or billions in the worst case scenarios—unleashing chaos and suffering on an unprecedented scale, all to pad a few corporate bottom lines.[3]

Yet for as long as it's been in the public consciousness, climate change has masqueraded, like other environmental problems, as a fight without enemies—as the old Pogo cartoon mourns, with the titular character staring out at a field of litter, "We have met the enemy and he is us."

Demand shapes supply, so we're all a tiny bit complicit in fossil fuels' toxic excavation. These companies and their products are ubiquitous. That we all use them has been a powerful defense for the companies profiting from them: energy executives spare no expense painting shareholder and public interest as one in the same. "Very few aspects of modern life aren't touched in some way by natural gas and oil," a shiny ad campaign from the American Petroleum Institute argues. "Thousands of products made from natural gas and oil make life healthier, safer, more comfortable

---

3   David Wallace-Wells, "UN Says Climate Genocide Is Coming. It's Actually Worse Than That," *New York Magazine*, October 10, 2018.

and more enjoyable ... They support creativity, help us manage our environment and think beyond ourselves."[4]

The strategy has worked, shifting focus away from the obvious: the first step to preventing catastrophic climate breakdown is to keep the fossil fuels that cause it in the ground, as Indigenous-led fights against projects like the Dakota Access and Keystone XL pipelines have argued.

Potentially trillions of dollars' worth of fossil fuel profits—stranded coal, oil, and gas assets—will have to go unrealized. The industry's legendary profitability is far more fragile than it looks. The moment world powers make credible commitments to slash carbon emissions, the stock value of oil will crash, likely precipitating a global economic crisis if we don't plan for it. We have met the enemy and he is a few hundred fabulously wealthy executives.

The inflated value of these companies is premised on a promise to kill. Prioritizing the lives of billions means seizing public control of the energy economy and assuring a just transition that improves people's lives, with a special focus on assisting fossil industry workers and the frontline communities that have been hardest hit by extraction. For ethical and practical reasons, a just transition also requires naming and shaming our enemies, focusing the climate movement's rage where it belongs: on fossil fuel CEOs and private utility executives.

---

4   American Petroleum Institute, "Energy Is Powering Manufacturing," api.org.

The debate over California's wildfires represents a break with usually diffuse chains of responsibility. PG&E, the utility that skimped on maintenance to fatten shareholder dividends, didn't cause every single one of the recent fires, but state investigators have found that they caused a lot of them. "There's a clear-cut pattern here: that PG&E is starting these fires," US District Judge William Alsup told company lawyers at a hearing early in 2019, drawing on the state's inverse condemnation laws. "Does the judge just turn a blind eye and say, 'PG&E, continue business as usual, continue to kill people'?"[5]

PG&E doesn't extract fossil fuels itself. But what made it responsible for so many wildfires is what makes companies like ExxonMobil responsible for the climate crisis: neglecting the public good with reckless energy operations for the sake of profit. During the Camp Fire, the utility declined to shut off power lines despite encroaching flames. In the years prior, it diverted $100 million from its safety and operations budget into executive bonuses and investor payouts, and spent $5 billion on shareholder dividends while delaying infrastructure upgrades that it knew were desperately needed. The same logic applies to fossil fuel producers. When shareholders' interests are the priority, then investing in new drilling and stock buybacks that offer the quickest buck isn't just more profitable for them than doubling down

5   Joel Rosenblatt, "PG&E Judge Sees a 'Clear-Cut Pattern' of Utility Starting Fires," bloomberg.com, January 31, 2019.

on renewables—it's a mission handed down from on high. Left unchallenged, it will result in catastrophe.

Dismal Science

By 2050, projected new oil and gas development in the United States—barring new regulations or a drastic change in oil prices—could unlock enough carbon to release the equivalent of the lifetime emissions of 1,000 coal-fired power plants. (In 2017, the United States had 359 coal plants.) And no country is planning to grow fossil extraction faster than the United States. Most new extraction is slated to happen in the Permian Basin in Texas and New Mexico and the Appalachian Basin in Ohio, Pennsylvania, and West Virginia. They won't stop there, either. Fossil fuel companies are constantly hunting for new reserves and new ways to extract from them. After the United States lifted an export ban in 2015, it's now increasingly exporting oil—and carbon pollution—to other countries.

The Intergovernmental Panel on Climate Change outlines a different to-do list. To cap warming at 1.5° Celsius, global coal, oil, and natural gas usage will have to decline, respectively, by 97, 87, and 74 percent, by 2050.[6] Decline should happen fastest in rich countries like the United States, which can afford a rapid transition off

---

6 V. Masson-Delmotte et al., "Summary for Policymakers," Intergovernmental Panel on Climate Change, October 8, 2018, ipcc.ch.

incumbent fuels. As we'll discuss in later chapters, that involves dramatically scaling up renewable energy, electrifying most energy use, and decarbonizing carbon-intensive sectors like agriculture and transportation.

The problem is, even as solar and wind have gotten cheaper and more widespread, the *proportion* of energy they generate nationwide has increased only slightly.[7] Good energy isn't displacing enough of the bad—it's just adding more. We need to stop the bad directly. This is especially true globally, where overall renewables are just adding clean power on top of dirty. Because carbon knows no borders, "net-zero" emissions at home won't mean much if exports continue. How could a radical Green New Deal leverage US policymaking to knee-cap the fossil fuel industry beyond our borders?

In economic parlance, emissions reductions measures generally fall into two buckets: supply-side policies, which deal with energy production, and demand-side policies dealing with its consumption. In the climate context, supply refers quite literally to the supply of fossil fuels, and restrictive supply-side policies limit emissions at their source in wells and mines through measures like fracking bans. Such policies would also phase out subsidies that encourage coal, oil, and gas development. Demand-side policies include successful measures like pro-renewable energy regulations ("renewable portfolio standards") and

---

7 "Short-Term Energy Outlook," US Energy Information Administration, June 11, 2019, eia.gov.

government procurement. Most controversially, demand-side policy involves tweaking energy consumption. The most hotly contested issue here is a carbon tax.

Pricing carbon would help. In the United States, it would encourage cleaner energy use where it's affordable and available, and help shape firms' long-term investments, like making sure any new company cars bought are electric. Border carbon adjustments would help prevent firms from moving their carbon-fueled production outside the United States, only to send carbon-rich products back into the country through trade.

But subtle market signals can only do so much. A carbon price low enough to be politically viable won't be high enough to transform global energy markets. According to the radicals at the Organization for Economic Co-operation and Development, most of the carbon fees that have been put into place are far too low to make a dent in emissions.[8] Meanwhile, as France's Yellow Vest protests show, forcing citizens to shoulder the cost of decarbonization is understandably unpopular when the context is austerity, shrinking taxes on the rich—whose consumption causes disproportionate pollution—and a lack of available and affordable no-carbon alternatives.

The Green New Deal isn't averse to market signals—but it will take public involvement in markets further than neoliberals dream. The kinds of public finance,

8 *Effective Carbon Pricing Rates 2018: Pricing Carbon Emissions Through Taxes and Emissions Trading* (OECD Publishing 2018).

procurement policies, pro-innovation research funds, and other measures that we have in mind are far stronger than centrists' proposed nudges. For neither a carbon price, nor a fuller suite of policies addressing the demand and supply of clean energy, is a substitute for direct, public regulations to simply keep the carbon buried.

In the United States, restrictive supply-side action has been a taboo for almost everyone except climate and environmental justice groups, who have long called for just that.

Economists Fergus Green and Richard Denniss write that policymakers have overemphasized efforts to limit demand for greenhouse gases with carbon taxes and cap-and-trade regimes, and that they have stayed "remarkably silent" on supply-side instruments.[9] Policymakers' reluctance to adopt restrictive supply side policies deprives us of critical tools for fighting climate disruption. Focusing exclusively on demand avoids attacking fossil fuel companies' core product, and more importantly fossil political power, head-on. That's a mistake a radical Green New Deal won't make.

California Oil Über Alles

With fires transforming its verdant hills into ashy grave-yards, smokestacks still belching carbon in poor

---

9   Fergus Green and Richard Denniss, "Cutting with Both Arms of the Scissors: The Economic and Political Case for Restrictive Supply-Side Climate Policies," Climate Change 150: 1–2, 2018, pp. 73–87.

neighborhoods, and solar panels proliferating, California's contradictions offer a glimpse into the possible future of American climate politics. For all of California's success with renewables, it also reveals the limits of lopsided demand-only policies.

In 2016, California met its target of getting emissions below 1990 levels four years early.[10] It's battled the White House in the courts to hold onto its ambitious fuel standards, which have made California home to half of the country's zero-carbon vehicles.[11] The state has had a cap-and-trade program to reduce emissions in place since 2012. While it hasn't significantly reduced emissions and has left much of the polluting industry in poor and racialized communities untouched, revenue from that program has directed funds into a panoply of green jobs programs and resiliency improvements to frontline communities. Just before leaving office, former Governor Jerry Brown signed a bill mandating that the state's electricity sector run 60 percent on renewables by 2030 and 100 percent on zero-carbon energy by 2045.[12] These changes haven't come out of the kindness of politicians' hearts—Brown

---

10 David Baker, "California Slashes Emissions, Hits Major Greenhouse Gas Goal Years Early," *San Francisco Chronicle*, July 11, 2018.

11 Aarian Marshall, "California Says 'Nope' to the EPA's Car Emissions Rules," wired.com, October 4, 2018.

12 David Roberts, "California Just Adopted Its Boldest Energy Target Yet: 100% Clean Electricity," vox.com, September 10, 2018.

and others are responding to the state's muscular climate and environmental justice movements.

These movements are rooted in the low-income communities of color that have refineries and fracking wells in their backyards. As organizers there are well aware, the state remains a major oil and gas producer. While anointing himself America's Trump-era ambassador to the world on US climate policy, Brown approved over 21,000 new permits for oil and gas drilling. California continues to subsidize this fossil extraction. It hands over land through lease approvals and other forms of state aid. And its enhanced oil recovery tax credit allows oil producers to write off drilling costs, in addition to federal tax breaks; in 2018, Chevron paid a negative 4 percent federal tax rate, receiving $181 million in rebates. That solar panels are popping up on Golden State rooftops isn't much solace when the Chevron plant in your backyard is still giving your kids asthma.

If California were to cut off its fossil fuel supply, at least some of it would be replaced by fuel from elsewhere. That's the argument of oil and gas lobbyists in the region. "Every barrel of oil not produced in California will be replaced by a barrel produced and shipped in from a region that doesn't have our state's stringent environmental laws," said Catherine Reheis-Boyd, president of the Western States Petroleum Association.[13]

---

13   Paul Rogers, "California Passes Bill to Block Trump's Offshore Drilling Plans," *Mercury News*, August 28, 2018.

But supply and demand influence one another: Cutting supply reshapes demand. The Stockholm Environment Institute reports that each barrel of oil left undeveloped in California would reduce global oil consumption by anywhere from 0.2 to 0.6 barrels, reducing global carbon emissions. If the state were to halve its oil production—to around 100 million barrels per year—the net carbon savings could range from 8 million to 24 million tons of CO_2 annually—the equivalent of taking as many as 4.7 million cars off the road every year.[14]

To be sure, supply restrictions also raise fuel prices. But because California already has strong renewable energy mandates, the technology and skills are there to accelerate the shift away from fossil fuels without risking a return to dirtier and less cost-efficient sources like coal or placing an undue financial burden on working-class households. Supply-side policies could make a sizable impact on both global emissions and the health of communities close to drill sites and refineries. Moving supply and demand *together* should be the strategy of a public-sector-led energy transition, finally listening to the common sense logic environmental justice groups in California and elsewhere have pushed for decades: We need alternatives to our dirty energy regime, and there is no alternative to stopping emissions at their source.

---

14 Peter Erickson et al., "Limiting Fossil Fuel Production as the Next Big Step in Climate Policy," *Nature Climate Change* 8 (2018), pp. 1037–43; "Greenhouse Gas Equivalencies Calculator," EPA, December 2018, epa.gov/energy/greenhouse-gas-equivalencies-calculator.

There's a long way to go. Despite presiding over murderous wildfires to appease shareholders, PG&E benefits from ample state support. At the time of writing, the utility is on the hook for some $30 billion in damages from the 2017 and 2018 fire seasons, plus lawsuits from survivors, local governments, and insurance companies. Despite the efforts of many California legislators and the notoriously industry-friendly California Public Utilities Commission, PG&E filed for Chapter 11 bankruptcy in January 2019. It can pass the cost of what's owed down to ratepayers in the form of higher utility bills—even for the people whose homes were incinerated and whose relatives perished. Governor Gavin Newsom urged legislators to change the laws to release PG&E and other utilities from much of their liability, foisting more of the burden onto ordinary Californians; in July 2019, he signed a hastily pushed-through bill that will see ratepayers pay $10.5 billion to bailout state utilities for the next 15 years, and cap how much the company could be made to pay for future disasters.[15] PG&E investors cheered. All this good-will toward it isn't an accident: the utility spent over $11.8 million on lobbying during the post-fire 2017–18 state legislative session.[16]

---

15 Taryn Luna, "Utility customers will pay $10.5 billion for California wildfire costs under bill sent to Newsom," *Los Angeles Times*, July 11, 2019.

16 Wes Venteicher and Sophia Bollag, "As California Wildfires Grew, so Did PG&E Lobbying Spending," *Sacramento Bee*, February 2, 2019.

The company's downward spiral has prompted a wider conversation about whether it deserved to exist at all. Legislators floated the idea of breaking up PG&E into various entities. Furious ratepayers joined with climate, environmental justice groups, and local chapters of the Democratic Socialists of America to flood usually sleepy regulatory meetings in opposition to a bailout and demanding an alternative: public ownership. Facing pressure, even Newsom put the idea of a state takeover on the table before making city and state takeovers more difficult with the bailout legislation passed in the summer of 2019, which will require the CPUC to sign-off on any ownership change.

"Our current model is only protecting PG&E shareholders. We have no say in the process," said Jessica Tovar, an organizer with the Local Clean Energy Alliance. "We have a utility that has operated dirty fossil-fueled power plants in primarily low-income communities of color for decades. So many people have died of cancer in this community. This is how a corporate monopoly functions: on the backs of the poorest people."[17]

Campaigns to bring private utilities under public ownership have also taken off in Providence, Boston, Boulder, Chicago, and elsewhere. Nationally, the Democratic Socialists of America's Ecosocialist working group centers such campaigns as a major initiative.

---

17   Conversation with Kate Aronoff, February 1, 2019.

There have also been grassroots efforts to bring democratic accountability to moribund public utilities that are run as poorly or even worse than their private counterparts. Climate organizers want to seize control of the New York Power Authority and build and generate power from its own wind turbines, giving the state a public option for renewable energy. In rural parts of the country, electric cooperative members are pushing to return those institutions to their directly democratic roots. From New York to Oklahoma to California, a Green New Deal will make private utilities public, and make public utilities better.

Separate Fossil and State

Like the Paris Agreement, the Green New Deal resolution introduced by Representative Alexandria Ocasio-Cortez (D-NY) and Senator Ed Markey (D-MA) didn't mention fossil fuels by name. Policies inspired by the Green New Deal should be explicit: without a frontal assault on the industry's power, we'll never make fast enough progress. Keenly aware of that fact, the masters of today's fossil energy universe are fighting like hell to prevent large-scale action.

Thanks to prolific lobbying and campaign contributions, fossil fuel producers collect $20.5 billion in direct state and federal subsidies from the United States each year. That figure doesn't account for the billions more the

Pentagon and State Department spend securing US companies' access to energy supplies and markets abroad through wars and diplomacy. Globally, the IMF has estimated that the full, unpaid social and environmental cost of burning fossil fuels amounts to $5.2 trillion in subsidies—about 6.5 percent of global GDP. Handouts to the fossil fuel industry are so extensive that the Stockholm Environment Institute has estimated that as much as half of new oil and gas development would be unprofitable without them.[18] These same corporate executives are also waging war on climate policies a fraction as ambitious as a radical Green New Deal.

As political scientist Leah Stokes has documented, state by state, investor-owned utilities have used lobbying and astroturf campaigns to effectively seize control of regulators, defeating efforts to scale up renewables; the Koch brothers have played an especially crucial role. In many cases, these moves rolled back clean energy policies that had already been passed. We haven't lost decades of opportunity to decarbonize because people love fossil fuels and hate change. Rather, there was a concerted campaign by private interests to block progress. Fossil fuel companies and private utilities have even mounted successful primary

---

18   See David Roberts, "Friendly Policies Keep US Oil and Coal Afloat Far More Than We Thought," vox.com, July 26, 2018; David Coady et al., "Global Fossil Fuel Subsidies Remain Large: An Update Based on Country-Level Estimates," International Monetary Fund, May 2, 2019, imf.org.

challenges to politicians they deemed too friendly to wind and solar. Across red states, an unholy alliance of big oil, private utilities, and conservative. Republicans have delayed progress on clean energy.

Globally, PG&E and other utilities worked with fossil fuel producers in the Global Climate Coalition—an influential industry group—to spread disinformation about climate change throughout the 1990s. Today that resistance is sometimes subtler, but no less dangerous. Already, with the Green New Deal in the headlines, fossil fuel interests, centrist economists, and a smattering of Democratic and Republican politicians are backing a modest carbon tax that would exempt them from lawsuits and regulations, while failing to substantially cut emissions.

Exxon and Shell knew for decades about the threat of the crisis, thanks to cutting-edge research by company scientists. PG&E and other investor-owned utilities did too.[19] We can't trust either to change their business models within the timeline that science demands. Our modest hope is that a Green New Deal can finally bring about an epochal energy transition that's firmly in the public interest, not shareholders'. That means recasting energy as a potent ground for political struggle, just like finance or health care. So what's the energy equivalent to breaking

---

19 Karen Savage, "Inside the GCC: The Industry Group That Mobilized to Fight Global Climate Action," climateliabilitynews.org, April 25, 2019; "1989 GCC Membership," climatefiles.com.

up the Wall Street banks and instituting free public health care? Public ownership of energy.

Toward Public Energy

We don't need fossil fuel companies, and—in the long run—we don't need fossil fuels at all. We do need electric utilities. In the case of fossil fuel producers, aligning their business model with the public interest means euthanizing them as quickly as possible. For utilities, it means excising the profit motive and bringing these institutions under democratic control so they can fulfill what should be their only mission: guaranteeing clean, cheap, or even free power to the people they serve. As anyone familiar with Saudi Aramco or today's coal-loving Rural Electric Cooperatives can tell you, public ownership—whether by the state or by ratepayers—is no fast track to decarbonization. The majority of the world's fossil fuel resources are under state ownership, along with 62 percent of installed electric generation capacity. Unsurprisingly, broader dynamics in energy markets are reflected in state-owned utilities, which have dramatically increased their investments in renewables over the last several years, while continuing to account for more than half of the world's coal-fired power plants, according to the Organization for Economic Co-operation and Development.[20]

---

20 Andrew Prag et al., "State-owned enterprises and the low-carbon transition—environment working paper No.129," OECD, April 25, 2018, oecd.org.

Many other changes are needed, too. The private-sector-friendly design of existing clean energy subsidies, for instance, makes it difficult for US public institutions to reap the benefits of tax credits for renewables, making serious innovation there difficult. Ditching shareholders is no panacea. But it opens doors to a zero-carbon world that private ownership would leave firmly locked.

The transition to public ownership and ensuing decarbonization is a necessarily different process for fossil fuel producers and investor-owned utilities, with distinct implications. Let's go through each in turn.

Fossil Fuel Producers

As discussed above, fossil fuel company valuations are wildly inflated, reflecting the value of profits that can't be realized without locking in runaway climate catastrophe. A necessary precursor to bringing them under public ownership is valuing them properly, by constraining their ability to explore and mine for endless amounts of deadly new supply. Any climate policy that would level the playing field for renewables would leave the industry and its supporters scrambling for a rescue plan. If and when those stocks are devalued by some mix of markets and policy, the answer isn't to bail them out and treat them as too big to fail, but to buy them out. The US government can bring US-based fossil fuel companies under public ownership by buying up 51 percent of their shares and then quickly curtailing production.

How much asset stranding is inevitable is up for debate. Market forces alone can't keep a critical mass of fossil fuels in the ground—particularly in a market that's so manifestly unfree, loaded up with subsidies for incumbent fuels in the name of national security. Renewables getting cheaper hasn't been particularly worrying for oil and gas companies. Supply-side policies like those discussed above can finally make them sweat, particularly if paired with a re-introduction of the crude oil export ban to cut off access to markets abroad.

A managed decline further ensures that workers in the fossil fuel industry and the communities that have been built up around it aren't left to the whims of the market. We know what happens otherwise: fossil fuel companies will declare bankruptcy and screw over their workers' health care and pensions, like flailing coal companies have in Appalachia. As we detail in the next chapter, workers and the communities they belong to deserve far better. Managed decline would be a saving grace for pensioners, too, whose livelihoods are now bound up with some of the world's most toxic companies. By skillfully managing the fossil fuel industry's liquidation, a Green New Deal can ensure that those pensions continue paying out and are funneled into safe, productive investments that drive the transition—a twenty-first-century version of the New Deal's Reconstruction Finance Corporation.

Short of full nationalization, there's plenty of common sense policies that can lay the groundwork for public ownership, limit drilling—and even make dirty energy executives see public takeover as a preferable option to bankruptcy. Ending fossil fuel subsidies would help renewables compete and free up tens of billions of dollars a year for greener uses. Establishing buffer zones between drill sites and homes, playgrounds, hospitals, and other sensitive areas could go a long way, too. When a now-stalled bill to ban drilling operations within 2,500 feet of such places passed through a California Assembly committee, stock sell-offs in two oil and gas companies collapsed their prices by around 15 and 10 percent, respectively. As the CEO of one of those companies told nervous investors on a quarterly earnings call, "It just spooked everyone."[21]

Electric Utilities

In the United States, electric utilities are variously owned by shareholders, state and local governments, and—in some of the country's most conservative parts—by the roughly 42 million "member-owners" of rural electric cooperatives, one of the longest living legacies of the original New Deal, created to fill the gap left by the private

21 HFI Research, "This California Resources Sell-Off Is Unwarranted," seekingalpha.com, April 25, 2019, seekingalpha.com; "AB-345 Oil and Gas: Operations: Location Restrictions," California Legislative Information, April 30, 2019, leginfo.legislature.ca.gov; "Circle Property (CRC) Q1 2019 Earnings Call Transcript," *The Motley Fool*, May 3, 2019, fool.com.

sector's failure to extend power lines to the rural poor. Several states have programs called Community Choice Aggregation, which essentially allow ratepayers to collectively bargain for fairer rates and power procurement. Such arrangements in California alone serve 2.6 million people. Nebraska's grid is entirely state-run by the Nebraska Public Power District. The Los Angeles Department of Power and Water serves up water and electricity to 4 million residents and businesses throughout Los Angeles. From Hammond, Wisconsin to Jacksonville, Florida to Lubbock, Texas, public power is familiar to Americans across the political spectrum. While the Right smears modest tax hikes as a slippery slope to Stalinism, plenty of registered Republicans already own the means of energy production.

The residents of Winter Park, Florida, took back their electricity from shareholders in 2005. After an adjustment period—rates went up initially—ratepayers now get cheaper and more reliable power, making about $5 million in annual profits that gets funneled into improving service and safety, not payouts to investors. Like the New Deal's electrification programs, benefits from a push for scaling up clean, public power can go well beyond rates and reliability. In North Carolina, the Roanoke Electric Cooperative has sponsored a Sustainable Forestry and African American Land Retention Program, assisting 117 landowners with everything from financial support to timber management.

"Members must be at the center of every activity we do on a daily basis," CEO Curtis Wynn says. Accordingly, the coop holds monthly "Straight Talk" forums in each of the counties where it operates for member-owners to hear updates and discuss what's working and what's not. Among the initiatives to emerge from the forums have been a slew of energy efficiency programs.[22]

While we shouldn't underestimate investor-owned utilities' capacity to polarize any issue, we should question Republicans' and cautious Democrats' assertion that public ownership is a third rail issue; most people harbor no love for their electric utility, let alone their executives. The biggest barrier to putting investor-owned utilities into public hands will be those utilities themselves and their gargantuan lobby.

So how do we do it? Let's start with PG&E. Johanna Bozuwa, of the Democracy Collaborative—which has done pioneering work around public energy ownership— wrote just after the company's bankruptcy declaration that, "With the company's value dropping precipitously, this is a key moment for the state to step in, take over, and design a utility system that centers affordability, reliability, resiliency and leadership on climate change."[23] With stock

---

22   Grant Williams, "Community Power: Fighting to Remain in Rural America II," colabradio.mit.edu, November 8, 2016; Kate Aronoff, "Bringing Power to the People: The Unlikely Case for Utility Populism," *Dissent*, Summer 2017, dissentmagazine.org.

23   Johanna Bozuwa, "Public Takeover of PG&E: A Radically

values low, California can buy a controlling share in PG&E for a steep discount. State-owned regional grid operators could make power delivery more responsive to local needs and conditions, and more nimble to respond to disasters when they occur. Instead of money flowing to shareholders and executive bonuses, it'd be reinvested back into efficiency upgrades, renewable capacity, electrification (for transportation, especially), and lower rates.

There are other paths, too. As a plan for a Green New Deal gained momentum in Maine, lawmakers spurred on by a statewide organizing and legislative push weighed replacing its two monopoly electric utilities with a single, publicly owned power provider. In Boulder, Colorado, voters moved to displace Xcel Energy with a public utility several years ago, though the company has stymied municipalization through court proceedings. We should expect any investor-owned utility to put up just as big a fight. Like the Rural Electrification Administration, a Green New Deal could facilitate bottom-up efforts for public power with federal funds and technical assistance.

Renewable power today faces a situation not unlike that which faced electricity in general during the Great Depression: the private sector isn't providing what's needed. Considering the urgency of a massive transition to renewable energy, what's so instructive about the New Deal's public power initiatives is their emphasis on

Common-Sense Proposal," localcleanenergy.org, January 17, 2019.

democratic planning as a means to get things done at scale: having established a broad set of criteria for which communities were eligible to apply for loans through the Rural Electrification Administration, administrators let communities do the work of deciding whether they wanted power lines. "The immediate and tangible results will be to bring electricity to a large proportion of American farms, to stimulate employment and manufacturing, and to raise living standards in rural communities," Rural Electrification Administration head Morris L. Cooke wrote in 1938. "The intangible values—building self-reliance and training leaders in every community—should prove no less satisfying."[24]

#Rex4Hague

Fossil fuel executives in particular should consider themselves lucky if all we do is take their companies. They should be tried for crimes against humanity.

On top of the climate-related deaths they cause, the wide range of effects of burning fossil fuels—air pollution, indoor smoke, occupational hazards, and cancerous agents—kill nearly 5 million people a year. By 2030, annual climate and carbon-related deaths are expected to reach nearly 6 million. That's the rough equivalent of one

---

24 Morris Llewellyn Cooke, "Electricity Goes to the Country," xroads.virginia.edu, September 1936.

Holocaust every year, which in just a decade could surpass the total number of people killed in World War II. Yet as we've detailed, the individuals at the helm of fossil fuel companies each day choose to seek out new reserves to burn as quickly as possible and to use every possible tool to sabotage regulatory action while knowing full well the deadly consequences.

Fossil fuel executives' behavior constitutes a Crime Against Humanity in the classical sense: "a widespread or systematic attack directed against any civilian population, with knowledge of the attack," including murder and extermination. Unlike genocide, the UN clarifies, in the case of crimes against humanity, "it is not necessary to prove that there is an overall specific intent," clarifying that the perpetrator must act "with knowledge of the attack against the civilian population and that his/her action is part of that attack."[25]

They may not have intended to destroy the world as we know it. And climate change may not look like the kinds of attacks we're used to. But they've known what their industry is doing to the planet for a long time.

To narrow the field of potential indictments, we might

---

25 "Rome Statute of the International Criminal Court: Part 2. Jurisdiction, Admissibility and Applicable Law," International Criminal Court, July 17, 1998, icc-cpi.int/nr/rdonlyres/ea9aeff7-5752-4f84-be94-0a655eb30e16/0/rome_statute_english.pdf; "Definitions: Crimes against Humanity," United Nations Office on Genocide Prevention and the Responsibility to Protect, un.org/en/genocideprevention/crimes-against-humanity.shtml.

start with ExxonMobil executives—particularly good targets given that there's been extensive documentation proving that the company's top brass knew about and then covered up the existence of climate change, even as they fortified their supply chains against climate impacts.

The legal hurdles to making such trials happen would be substantial. If the Nuremberg Trials were outside the box for international law at the time, trying fossil fuel executives for crimes against humanity might well be in the stratosphere. Royal Dutch Shell is based in the Netherlands and, unlike the United States, is a party to the Rome Statute. In order for its executives to be tried for crimes against humanity, an International Criminal Court (ICC) prosecutor would need to open an investigation to determine whether domestic courts in the Netherlands had failed to hold the offending parties accountable. If not, the prosecutor could then bring an indictment before the ICC, which would hear the case. The Dutch government could alternately refer the case to the court itself. Plenty of countries have crimes against humanity statutes, though, so a trial wouldn't necessarily have to happen under the notoriously sluggish auspices of the ICC. Climate-vulnerable countries in the Global South could bring suits against American and European fossil fuel companies. Options abound.

After all, the Nuremberg trials were themselves a kind of experimentation, wherein Allied forces effectively tested a new legal doctrine crafted to fit the specific atrocities committed by Axis forces, for which there was no established legal framework. Confronting climate change—the greatest existential threat the world has ever known—demands thinking no less creative.

And however much faith you place in bodies like the ICC, a push to try fossil fuel executives for crimes against humanity could channel some much-needed populist rage at the climate's 1 percent and render them persona non grata in respectable society—let alone Congress or the UN, where they today enjoy broad access. Making people like Exxon CEO Darren Woods or Shell CEO Ben van Beurden widely reviled would put names and faces to a problem too often discussed in the abstract.[26] The climate fight has clear villains. It's long past time to drag their reputations through the mud and subject these executives to at least the same level of public scrutiny that banking CEOs like Jamie Dimon and Lloyd Blankfein have faced after the financial crisis. Ideally, some of them will actually be held accountable.

None of these lengthy bureaucratic processes will kick off without massive public pressure, which in itself could bear fruit beyond indictments. Exciting as these trials might be, the most pressing work ahead is to decarbonize the global economy. If in the long run we hope to bring fossil fuel executives to court, the road there should make

---

26 Information about Darren Woods and Ben van Beurden is available at corporate.exxonmobile.com and shell.com/about-us, respectively.

sure that their destructive companies are taken out of private hands and run in the public interest—and wound down as quickly as possible, with the first priority being to ensure a dignified quality of life for workers and their communities.[27]

The climate crisis has long been framed as an issue of either techno-utopian tinkering, entrusting a few billionaires to save the day, or of collective self-sacrifice—us versus us. Have fewer children. Buy organic. Drive less. Amid all the carbon shaming, it's worth recalling Occupy Wall Street's most enduring slogan: the 99 percent versus the 1 percent. If we didn't write ourselves subprime mortgages and we didn't on a whim decide to saddle ourselves with six figures worth of student debt, *we* certainly didn't wreck the planet. They did.

Whether meant to keep pesky English villagers from slagging off at work in watermill-powered factories along the Thames, or to cut off the many choke points where workers could disrupt coal mining and distribution, previous energy transitions have mainly served the purpose of consolidating power and profits among the already wealthy. As we name our enemies, we can cut across the jobs versus environment myth that pits those who stand to benefit most from this transition against one another.

27 Carla Skandier, "Nationalize the Fossil Fuel Industry," *In These Times*, November 17, 2017.

Dividing the 99 percent against itself is capitalism's favorite and most effective trick; it was coal executives, after all, who during Reconstruction began bussing in Black strikebreakers—lured to those jobs under false pretenses—in order to undermine labor militancy and multiracial solidarity, training white miners' animosity on potential comrades instead of the bosses screwing them both over. As one mine superintendent put it bluntly, the goal was to make the issue "one of race between the white and colored miners, and not one of wages or conditions of work between the coal companies and their employees."[28]

The losers of a Green New Deal are energy companies and their shareholders. And today's fossil fuel executives will be every bit as vicious defending their business model's right to exist as they were in trying to break up unions. The fact they're eager to obscure? The winners of a radical Green New Deal are everyone else.

---

28 Quintard Taylor, *The Forging of a Black Community: Seattle's Central District From 1870 through the Civil Rights Era* (University of Washington Press 1994), pp. 27, 68.

2

STRIKE FOR SUNSHINE

We have a powerful enemy in the form of fossil capital. To defeat it, we need a powerful low-carbon labor movement.

Organized labor has historically played a key role keeping capital in check and pushing for the expansion of public goods. But since the environmental legislation of the 1970s, the Right has pitted labor against the environment, driving a wedge between two of capital's most significant twentieth-century challengers. Since then, the Right has bludgeoned every proposed environmental action with the threat of lost jobs, even as they gut worker protections. Unfortunately, it's been a winning strategy. The Right's anti-labor politics paradoxically make workers more dependent on the jobs they have and more anxious about the prospect of instability.

Progressives have tried to reassure workers that they won't pay for environmental protection with their livelihoods. "Green jobs" has been the refrain of environmental policy for years. It was a major slogan of Barack Obama's 2008 campaign: advisor Van Jones argued that a green jobs program could simultaneously address climate change, income inequality, and racial inequality. Yet Obama's green jobs policies ultimately consisted of funding for worker training and an effective but temporary home weatherization program.

Ten years later, decarbonization will have to happen much faster. The transition could be brutal for workers in the fossil fuel and related industries—but it doesn't have to be. Climate action doesn't have to mean lost jobs—it can mean better work for most people than what's on offer today. Mere job training, however, isn't going to cut it. Beyond high-quality retraining and new work in the clean energy sector, a just transition for labor would transform work more broadly and increase the power of all workers in relation to their bosses, by offering real alternatives to bad jobs and strengthening labor's right to organize.

To win all this, workers themselves will have to fight for it. That means we need a long-term vision that delivers material improvements along the way, building worker power step by step.

The Green New Deal resolution moves in this direction, calling for job training as well as high-quality union jobs, with comparable wages and benefits for affected workers. What most distinguishes it from previous green jobs schemes is the job guarantee—the idea that the government will provide a job to whoever wants one. The guarantee part is crucial. It represents a commitment to leaving no one behind amidst economic transformation and climate chaos. It also dramatically improves labor's position by raising the floor for bargaining, providing workers with exit options, and tightening the labor market, all of which make it possible to fight harder for further change.

The original New Deal is still the landmark for worker protections and public sector employment in the United States. It shows what happens when the federal government offers people good work and protects their efforts to organize. Today, we need to go beyond the New Deal's job programs and undertake a deeper economic transition.

That means expanding our understanding of what green jobs are. They tend to be seen as directly related to energy production, whether upgrading the grid or building renewable energy infrastructure. But truly greening the economy requires more fundamental transformations. We argue for expanding the green job framework to center work that is already low-carbon: caring for people and the earth. Labor can remake the world along carbon-free lines—and different kinds of labor can help us live good, low-carbon lives. To win those things, we need labor's power.

Just Transitions

A familiar dynamic has developed around fights to "keep it in the ground," with workers building oil and gas pipelines arrayed against climate and Indigenous activists organizing to stop them. These fights recall earlier battles, like the loggers-versus-spotted-owl fights of the 1980s that produced the slogan "Are You an Environmentalist, or Do You Work for a Living?" But the dichotomy is a false one. As labor historian Trish Kahle observes, "environmental protections and labor protections have historically risen and fallen together."[1] And workers have often recognized that companies that treat the earth badly usually treat their workers badly, too.

Take coal miners. In 1968, Kahle recounts, a mining disaster killed seventy-eight coal miners, leading rank-and-file miner Jock Yablonski to challenge the union's incumbent president, Tony Boyle. As Yablonski asked, "What good is a union that reduces coal dust in the mines only to have miners and their families breathe pollutants in the air, drink pollutants in the water, and eat contaminated commodities?" He gave voice to a growing sentiment. In 1969, 60,000 miners took part in wildcat strikes focusing on safety issues, and 70,000 marched on the West Virginia capital to demand

---

1　Trish Kahle, "Take on the Fossil Fuel Bosses," *Jacobin*, March 14, 2019, jacobinmag.com.

protections against black lung disease. Yablonski narrowly lost the election—and was later murdered by Boyle's hitmen. After his death, a group called Miners for Democracy took up the struggle for health and environmental protections, proposing that miners who lost jobs to regulations be given union work restoring local land and infrastructure.[2]

Yet their power faded as energy giants bought up coal companies and crushed worker militancy. Coal companies have since slacked on safety measures and black lung disease has viciously resurged—yet Trump is poised to cut regulations still further. Giant companies blow the tops off mountains and tout the benefits of "clean coal," even though there's no such thing.

Meanwhile, there's plenty of work to be had in the oil and gas industry as US extraction has expanded: jobs are up 60 percent from 2004 to 2016 despite the recession. Though fewer than 5 percent of extractive industry workers were union members as of 2018, even non-unionized workers can make good money. There's a reason workers are skeptical that green jobs will be as lucrative.

Yet an early wave of blue-green alliances laid the foundations for addressing these challenges. In the 1970s and 1980s, Tony Mazzocchi, a leader in the Oil, Chemical and Atomic Workers International Union, argued for winding

---

2   Trish Kahle, "Austerity vs. the Planet: The Future of Labor Environmentalism," *Dissent*, Spring 2016, dissentmagazine.org.

down industries that harmed workers, environment, and society while taking steps to safeguard livelihoods. He proposed a revived GI Bill for atomic workers who would be left unemployed by nuclear disarmament and a Superfund for fossil fuel workers. His vision was central to the idea of a just transition on which the Green New Deal draws—an economic transition that doesn't make workers pay, and that workers will fight for.

Jobs for All

The job guarantee is another such idea. It goes back to FDR's 1944 proposal for a Second Bill of Rights, known as the Economic Bill of Rights, which aimed to give a material foundation to the civil and political rights of the original. It called for the rights to "a good education," "adequate medical care," a "decent home," "protection from old age, sickness, accident, and unemployment," and a "useful and remunerative job in the industries or shops or farms or mines of the nation."

Its ambitious aims remain a worthy touchstone for the American Left. Yet there's a mismatch between the goods it declares people have a right to—health care, education—and the jobs they have a right to do—in mines, shops, and farms. What about the jobs in hospitals and schools that provide education and health care? The discrepancy is hardly limited to FDR. The archetypal worker has been a man in a hard hat or on the assembly line—not a teacher, nurse, or service worker, even as their numbers have grown.

Two decades after the New Deal, the idea of a job guarantee was at the heart of the Poor People's Campaign led by an increasingly radical Martin Luther King Jr. After King's death, his widow and political comrade Coretta Scott King carried on the fight, articulating a more transformative vision of work. As the historian David Stein observes, she wanted to create "jobs that would serve some human need." She emphasized health care, education, and quality of life over jobs "created with the profit-making motive."[3]

Her vision didn't come to pass. Instead of guaranteeing meaningful work to those without steady employment, the state imprisoned millions of people deemed "surplus" to capitalism's needs. As Ruth Wilson Gilmore shows, when economic growth began to falter in the 1960s, capitalists and homeowners revolted against their tax rates. The state lost its welfare mandate, but it still had money and capacity. It used them to build prisons rather than schools or public services. Gilmore is clear: "prison building was and is not the inevitable outcome."[4] It was a political choice. We can, and must, make a different one today.

---

3 David Stein, "Why Coretta Scott King Fought for a Job Guarantee," *Boston Review*, May 17, 2017.

4 Ruth Wilson Gilmore, *Golden Gulag: Prisons, Surplus, Crisis, and Opposition in Globalizing California* (University of California Press 2007), p. 88.

Though Donald Trump boasts about his job creation success, an estimated 16 million Americans are currently unemployed or underemployed. The economist Pavlina Tcherneva suggests that in 2017, around 11–16 million people would have taken advantage of a job guarantee.[5] What kinds of jobs would all those people do?

Under a radical Green New Deal, a job guarantee would offer low-carbon, socially valuable work—and there's no shortage of that. Every year, Americans do millions of hours of unpaid labor in food pantries and senior centers—including service mandated by courts, schools, or workfare. In the national parks alone, there are over 315,000 volunteers, compared to a mere 23,000 paid staff.[6] Other vital ecological care work is simply not being done at all. We don't need to make work—we need to pay for it.

The economic question is whether this work can be done profitably. Much of it, we submit, cannot. Eventually, doing meaningful, socially useful work will require a break with capitalism. We can start by drastically expanding the amount of work that's primarily oriented toward meeting ecological and human needs, not increasing profits.

5   Pavlina R. Tcherneva, "The Job Guarantee: Design, Jobs, and Implementation," Working Paper No. 902, Levy Economics Institute, 2018, p. 33.

6   National Park Service FAQs, nps.gov/aboutus/faqs.htm; National Park Service Budget Justifications 2019, nps.gov/aboutus/upload/FY2019-NPS-Budget-Justification.pdf.

Job guarantee advocates sometimes assure critics that it would supplement or stimulate private sector employment rather than crowding it out. But frankly, there are some jobs that ought to be crowded out. "Will you not be bewildered," the socialist William Morris once asked, "as I am, at the thought of the mass of things which no sane man could desire, but which our useless toil makes—and sells?" Work worth doing, Morris thought, had the "hope of rest, hope of product, hope of pleasure in the work itself." We should crowd out jobs that offer none of these—folding clothes in H&M or flipping burgers made from factory-farmed cattle—especially when their business model relies on wrecking the planet. A job guarantee would give workers options to leave socially and environmentally harmful jobs, and would strengthen the position of workers organizing in the private sector.

Shitty work also takes a toll on your soul. The great modernist writer Virginia Woolf once made a living from odd jobs of the kind then available to women—in her words, "addressing envelopes, reading to old ladies, making artificial flowers, teaching the alphabet to small children in a kindergarten." It was dull work, and usually poorly paid. "What still remains with me," she recalled afterward, "was the poison of fear and bitterness which those days bred in me." Then she inherited five hundred pounds a year from an aunt who fell off a horse in Bombay. It wasn't a fortune—about $40,000 today, a little more than the median individual income. But it set her free. "Watch in the spring sunshine," she wrote, "the stockbroker and the great barrister going indoors to make money and more money and more money when it is a fact that five hundred pounds a year will keep one alive in the sunshine."

A colonial inheritance isn't something to aspire to. But the freedom Woolf experienced should be available to all—and that's what a job guarantee can offer. In the 1930s, Lula Gordon, a Black woman living in San Antonio, wrote to FDR: "I was under the impression that the government or the WPA would give the Physical [sic] fit relief clients work. I have been praying for that time to come ... I have registered for a government job and when it opens up I want to take it." Gordon had long worked as a domestic servant and had been offered a job cleaning a white woman's home. Without other options, Gordon wrote, "I have to take the job in the private home or none." But she hoped for something else. "Will you please give me some work," her letter concluded.[7] A government job would offer an alternative to the intimate, racialized domination that usually comes with domestic servitude.

---

7 Cited in Evelyn Nakano Glenn, "From Servitude to Service Work: Historical Continuities in the Racial Division of Paid Reproductive Labor," *Signs*, 19:1–43 (1992), p. 13; originally in Julia Kirk Blackwelder, *Women of the Depression: Caste and Culture 1929–1939* (Texas A&M 1984), pp. 68–9.

Employers know this, too. During the New Deal, Southern politicians protested that Civil Works Administration wages were too high: Southern agriculture relied on Black workers who would plow the fields for five cents an hour, which they wouldn't do if the federal government were paying forty. Indeed, public sector jobs have long been important in countering the racial discrimination that makes Black and other workers of color "last hired, first fired." A job guarantee could help combat the rampant obstacles to decent employment for formerly incarcerated people. And it would help people escape abuse in families and households, which women, queer, and trans people are most likely to suffer.

The domination of the workplace still keeps most of us unfree. Bosses belittle and sexually harass workers, deny them bathroom breaks and vacation time, steal their wages, and drive them to exhaustion. But under capitalism, you have to work to live, so workers take what they can get. Real alternatives are essential. Only when workers can threaten to walk away can they build the power to fight back.

Building a New World

To decarbonize, we need to remake everything from how we travel to where we live. That entails a huge amount of work: retrofitting millions of existing buildings and constructing millions of units of no-carbon public housing, erecting a continent-spanning smart grid, and constructing vast networks of train lines, among other tasks. The Right has mocked the Green New Deal resolution's call to "retrofit every existing building in America" and rebuild American infrastructure as "insane," "unserious," and "unrealistic." But where do they think the highways came from?

The New Deal is famous for its public works projects. Workers hired under the Works Progress Administration constructed 651,000 miles of highway and 124,00 bridges, including the Oakland-San Francisco Bay Bridge and the Lincoln Tunnel. They built 125,000 public buildings, including 41,300 schools, and 469 airports. They built 8,000 parks, and 18,000 playgrounds and athletic fields. They built a multistate power system through the Tennessee Valley Authority.[8]

Today, we need to build fewer miles of roads and more miles of train tracks, fewer airports and more bus stations. We should dismantle oil derricks and pipelines. But the scale and ambition of these famous projects remind us of what's possible.

Discussions of this kind of scale-up often invoke not just the New Deal but "wartime mobilization"—the drastic increase in industrial capacity leading up to the US entry into World War II. Bill McKibben takes

---

8   Michael Hiltzik, *The New Deal: A Modern History* (Free Press 2011), p. 421.

inspiration from the "wholesale industrial retooling that was needed to build weapons and supply troops on a previously unprecedented scale," arguing that today we need to "build a hell of a lot of factories to turn out thousands of acres of solar panels, and wind turbines the length of football fields, and millions and millions of electric cars and buses."[9] Those projects are necessary— though we'd suggest more buses and fewer cars—and will create thousands of jobs for whose who now work in extractive industries.

UK Labour leader Jeremy Corbyn has echoed union leader Mazzocchi in calling for a GI Bill equivalent that would "guarantee that all energy workers are offered retraining, a new job on equivalent terms and conditions covered by collective agreements, and fully supported in their housing and income needs through transition."[10] We could do the same.

But building solar panels and wind turbines is a transitional strategy—not a model for a new economy. We can't just ramp up the production of "green" technology indefinitely. We need a plan for what comes next. After World War II, expanded productive capacity was restored to capitalists and redeployed toward mass production of consumer goods—with disastrous

9   Bill McKibben, "A World at War," *New Republic*, August 18, 2016.

10   John McDonnell, "A Green New Deal for the UK," *Jacobin*, May 30, 2019, jacobinmag.com.

environmental consequences. And although the war ended, military Keynesianism did not: military spending is still a major source of employment and economic stimulus. But we don't need to build solar panels forever—and we certainly don't need any more multi-billion-dollar military boondoggles. We do need to go all out for a decade or two to build a world that will last—a world of things that are functional and beautiful, a world of restored nature and communal luxury. And then we need to live in it.

Making a Life

What kind of work does living well require? Alexandria Ocasio-Cortez and Ed Markey's Green New Deal resolution calls for "high-quality health care; affordable, safe, and adequate housing; economic security; and clean water, clean air, healthy and affordable food, and access to nature." Both Republicans and climate wonks scoffed: what do health care and housing have to do with climate change? Weren't these just the "socialist wish list"?

In fact, the resolution got it exactly right. These aren't add-ons to the real climate program of clean energy production—they're essential to a new economy. We need more work that's oriented toward sustaining and improving life, human and nonhuman, in low-carbon ways. Hospitals and schools need to run on clean energy, of course, but care and education are inherently low-carbon.

The New Deal is often thought of as a Keynesian program for reinvigorating production. But as historians Salar Mohandesi and Emma Teitelman argue, it was also a program for social reproduction.[11] Amid the collapse of the world economy, millions struggled to survive: shantytowns sprang up, infant mortality rose drastically, and disease and suicide increased.

The federal government provided a lifeline in the form of direct relief and jobs created through an array of agencies. Teachers were among the first workers hired by the Federal Emergency Relief Agency, working in Emergency Nursery Schools and providing classes for adults in everything from basic literacy to general education. Other relief jobs were tailored to unemployed workers' skills: statisticians helped hospitals study disease; bookbinders helped libraries repair books; historians catalogued significant buildings. As the sculptor Gutzon Borglum wrote, the goal of the Civil Works Administration was "to make more livable our towns and cities, our schools more cheerful, our playgrounds and our parks a pride and a delight."[12] Like teaching and caring, repairing books and cataloguing buildings can be no-carbon work. In this spirit, Tcherneva calls for designing a job guarantee program as a "National Care Act," centering jobs that provide care for the

11 Salar Mohandesi and Emma Teitelman, "Without Reserves," in Tithi Bhattacharya (ed.), *Social Reproduction Theory* (Pluto Press 2017).

12 Quoted in Nick Taylor, *American-Made: The Enduring Legacy of the WPA: When FDR Put the Nation to Work* (Bantam 2008), p. 127.

environment and communities—for example, organizing after-school activities, working in community gardens, or running compost centers.[13]

From this perspective, proposals such as Medicare for All and College for All aren't distractions from decarbonization—they're part of a broader project about living a good life.

Public universities are already the largest employers in nine states; hospitals are the largest in another eleven. A drastic expansion of public higher education, on the scale of that in the 1960s, would give more people the chance to continue their education without going into life-destroying debt. It would also mean a huge number of new jobs— in teaching and research, but also in vital janitorial, food service, and administrative work.

Medicare for All could similarly mean the expansion of publicly funded work and with it, significant improvements in health care. Private hospitals realize profits just like any other company—by squeezing more labor out of fewer workers. The result is worse outcomes for patients, as health care workers have long emphasized. The crisis of care hits vulnerable patients the hardest. Pregnancy and childbirth kill Black people at nearly 3.5 times the rate of whites, for example; Black babies are twice as likely to die as white ones. New parents must have access to pre- and postpartum care regardless of race or class.

---

13   Tcherneva, "The Job Guarantee."

Federally funded childcare, meanwhile, would employ childcare workers at higher wages and give everyone time off—and not only to go to a different job. To paraphrase the Marxist feminist Silvia Federici, every parent is a working parent—and parents should have time for themselves, too.[14] Everyone should have access to quality mental health care, as the ongoing mental health crisis makes clear—a crisis likely to be exacerbated as a growing number of people watch their homes burn or neighbors die in hurricane gales. Making health care a public good would also make it possible for people to choose socially and ecologically beneficial work without worrying about losing their benefits. And providing public care of various kinds will lessen the burden of unwaged care work that still falls on women, and working-class women in particular.

The care crisis will only intensify as the country keeps aging. By 2030, all Boomers will have reached retirement age. We could be heading for an economic and social catastrophe of people in need of long-term care without the resources to pay for it. Under a radical Green New Deal, we could guarantee good care to the growing population of elderly, linking the well-being of younger generations faced with climate change to that of older ones faced with the crisis of care.

---

14   Silvia Federici and Jill Richards, "Every Woman Is a Working Woman: Silvia Federici interviewed by Jill Richards," *Boston Review*, December 19, 2018, bostonreview.net.

Care work can be rewarding, but it can also be tedious, emotionally bruising, and physically straining. It's real work, however nice "care" sounds. It is also intensely gendered and racialized. The vast majority of caregivers are women; a quarter of caretakers are immigrants, many undocumented. This work is unevenly regulated and its wages are much too low. But it's no less crucial for social and ecological well-being than that of solar panel installers. Better pay and social recognition are crucial for both building the no-carbon economy and addressing a division of labor that gives women and people of color the worst paid and lowest status jobs.

Caring for the Earth

We need to care for one another. Climate breakdown also demands that we take better care of the planet we live on.

The most famous example of an ecologically oriented jobs program is the New Deal's Civilian Conservation Corps (CCC). At its peak it employed over half a million men at a time—and only men. In total, between 1933 and 1941, it employed more than 3 million. CCC members prevented forest fires and fought them; they undertook flood control, disaster relief, soil conservation, and wildlife aid. They built recreational facilities—cabins, picnic tables, amphitheaters, and thousands of miles of hiking trails, on the principle that "Uncle Sam wants every worker to get the rest and relaxation necessary to send him back to his job doubly efficient." (We're okay with just the rest and relaxation.) Pay was lower than the standard union wage; CCC participants lived in barracks and worked long hours. Like other New Deal jobs programs, it was temporary.

Many of those elements persist in the CCC as it exists today—the California Conservation Corps. The program offers year-long positions to Californians from the ages of eighteen to twenty-five, touting the slogan "hard work, low pay, miserable conditions, and more!" Both the original and contemporary CCC treat conservation work as something that young people can do for a year or two before moving on to a real career. But why should we expect the work of caring for our planet to come with long hours, bad pay, and self-sacrifice? Why should it be something that you do only as a learning experience or as a stepping stone to a longer term job? We should treat these jobs as real work that you can do while living a real life.

A renewed, permanent version of the CCC could create new hiking trails and nature reserves in rural areas—and could also do more to care for ecosystems themselves. A new CCC could restore areas that have been damaged by industrial production, like the hundreds of Superfund sites awaiting cleanup. In places like West Virginia and Wyoming, former coal miners could turn abandoned coal mines into national parks dedicated to labor and environmental history. In cities, a CCC could employ people to plant trees and gardens amid miles of concrete—simultaneously improving quality of life, absorbing carbon, and keeping cities cooler amidst the heat waves to come.

The original CCC employed nearly 15,000 Indigenous people in the first six months and 85,000 overall; it also supported Indigenous self-rule. A revived version could be paired with a new program for Indigenous sovereignty and control over Indigenous lands. It should also draw on Indigenous knowledge, looking to Indigenous communities as leaders in ecological restoration and care. Indigenous scholar Nick Estes, for example, describes Water Protectors at Standing Rock as "*working* to protect their land and water."[15] We embrace the Red Nation's call for a Red Deal that includes multispecies caretaking, land, water, air, and animal restoration, and the enforcement of treaty rights, among other demands for environmental and social justice.[16] We could also take cues from programs to employ Indigenous workers in land management in Australia in recent years, which have been enormously beneficial both socially and ecologically.

Ecosystems do a lot of work to keep our planet habitable; we need to put in more work to keep them alive and flourishing in return. Restoration and rewilding can help

15   Nick Estes, *Our History Is the Future: Standing Rock versus the Dakota Access Pipeline and the Long Tradition of Indigenous Resistance* (Verso 2019), p. 49.

16   The Red Nation, "Call to Action: The Red Deal, Indigenous Action to Save Our Earth, June 19–20," therednation.org.

absorb a huge amount of carbon: plants absorb carbon dioxide and use sunlight to convert it into roots, leaves, and branches. Prairie grasslands are excellent carbon sinks, storing huge amounts of carbon in roots that stretch far underground. But much of America's prairie land has been converted into cattle feedlots, which dump greenhouse gases into the air in the form of—yes—cow burps. Restoring the stunning landscapes of the Great Plains would also draw down carbon.

Still, already-emitted carbon will wreak havoc for a long time. There will be more fires, more floods, more tornadoes, and more heat waves. We'll need more people trained to respond, capable of guiding large-scale evacuations and in some cases, long-term displacements. (Today, incarcerated people make up a third of California's firefighting force; in 2018, around 1,700 incarcerated people were paid a dollar an hour to fight the deadly fires that swept the state. Yet when they leave prison, many can't get firefighting jobs.)[17] We'll need construction workers to rebuild homes and neighborhoods, and social workers and therapists to help people put their lives back together.

Healthy ecosystems also protect human communities from extreme weather. In southeastern Louisiana, coastal wetlands are rapidly eroding as a result of a levee system

17 Annika Neklason, "California Is Running Out of Inmates to Fight Its Fires," *Atlantic*, December 7, 2017, theatlantic.com.

that disrupts the Mississippi delta and intensive fossil fuel activity along the coast. If current trends continue, one-third of existing coastal land will be gone by 2050. Thousands of miles of wetland ecosystems home to hundreds of species would be lost to the Gulf and over 2 million people forced to migrate. New Orleans would be significantly more vulnerable to hurricanes and flooding, threatening its survival. By contrast, restoring Louisiana's wetlands could employ thousands of former fossil-fuel workers to dismantle miles of gas pipelines that crisscross disappearing marshes, and to plant new vegetation.

Our current agricultural system doesn't include much care for the earth—and that should change. American agriculture is built to produce as much as possible as quickly as possible with as little labor as possible in fields organized like factories, owned by giant "family farmers" working in tandem with agribusiness companies to squeeze as much as they can out of land and labor, at high cost to both. Better farming, which uses a range of techniques to sequester carbon and sees the food system as embedded in broader ecosystems, would involve more—and more humane—human work close to the ground: careful pruning in orchards, tending to scarcer livestock that will eat farm scraps and provide natural fertilizer, and cultivating of plants that support the insects that pollinate crops, and feed birds and frogs. It would mean better systems for irrigating scarce water and flexible adaptations to extreme weather.

The conditions of agricultural work must also improve. Farming is often grueling, and farm workers are among the most exploited in the country. Around two-thirds are immigrants, mostly from Mexico and other Central American countries whose own agricultural sectors have been undermined by US trade policies. An estimated half are undocumented, leaving them at the mercy of hard-driving bosses. Their wages are exceedingly low, keeping food prices down so that other workers can get by on lower paychecks. This means that raising the wages of farm workers goes hand-in-hand with raising wages for workers more broadly.[18] Federal support for sustainable, carbon-sequestering farming can also tackle endemic poverty in rural communities. And while farming will always be hard, it doesn't have to be thankless.

Time for What We Will

Redefining work is crucial—but so is reducing it. That's long been a demand of the labor movement, which famously fought for the eight-hour day and the weekend. Early in the twentieth century, labor leader William Green thought imminent "the dawn of a new era—leisure for all."

Even some capitalists supported shorter hours: after all, workers needed time off to consume the goods they

18 Raj Patel and Jim Goodman, "A Green New Deal for Agriculture," *Jacobin*, April 4, 2019, jacobinmag.com.

produced. But Harvard economist Thomas Nixon Carver warned at the time that

> there is no reason for believing that more leisure would ever increase the desire for goods. It is quite possible that the leisure would be spent in the cultivation of the arts and graces of life; in visiting museums, libraries, and art galleries, or hikes, games and inexpensive amusements

which "would cut down the demand for the products of our wage-paying industries."[19] The trick was not to let leisure go too far—it should never replace work and consumption as the centers of life.

In the early days of the New Deal, Labor Secretary Frances Perkins supported a thirty-hour work week. But when business complained, "full-time full employment" was instead defined as forty hours a week. Later, wartime production locked in longer hours. Ultimately, the decision to stimulate consumption instead of promoting leisure was a way of avoiding deeper structural changes—to grow the pie rather than ask who was eating most of it. The environmental consequences have been dire. Today, the forty-hour week is still the standard, even though full-time work is hard for many to come by—and with wages

---

19 Benjamin Hunnicutt, *Free Time: The Forgotten American Dream* (Temple University Press 2013), p. 114.

stagnant, even forty hours often isn't enough to pay the bills. "One Job Should Be Enough," the slogan of striking hotel and grocery store workers, expresses the exhaustion of cobbling together a living across several part-time, low-wage jobs.

But under a radical Green New Deal, with efficiency gains and automation controlled by people rather than bosses, we could meet everyone's needs working far less than we currently do—and we should. Study after study shows that shorter workweeks lower carbon footprints—the shorter the better. To cut carbon, we need to work less and share the remaining work more evenly.

That would give people time to go to the theater or the movies, the club or the bar, to read or paint or become an underground hip hop sensation. With more time, we can learn how to do new things—take up surfing with the help of a publicly funded instructor or finally learn a new language. We can enjoy the arts and culture created by people employed by programs following in the model of the Works Progress Administration, which funded an efflorescence of cultural production, especially for the racialized working class. Singers and actors performed for communities around the country instead of just for the wealthy, while the Indian Arts and Crafts Board celebrated native folk art traditions. New Deal arts funding strengthened the Harlem Renaissance. It also helped launch the careers of Paul Robeson, the great Black Communist actor and singer, and of leading Abstract Expressionist painters like Jackson Pollock and Mark Rothko, both employed by the Works Progress Administration. That's what we call a creative economy.

Carbon-free leisure doesn't just mean wholesome hobbies like hiking and gardening—we're firm believers in eco-friendly hedonism. Give us time for long dinners with friends and plenty of organic wine; outdoor adventures enhanced by legal weed grown and harvested by well-paid agricultural workers; skinny-dipping in lakes that reflect moon and starlight.

From Coal Power to Union Power

We won't achieve any of this without revitalizing labor militancy. Labor's power has always come from its ability to bring business as usual to a halt. We need that power more than ever today, because business as usual threatens life on earth. Labor organizing can also mobilize working class communities, building powerful movements rather than accepting the divisions the boss tries to draw between workers and the public.

Past blue-green coalitions of environmentalists and unions have focused on workers in extractive industries. But a Green New Deal coalition would fight to make life better for working people more broadly. This isn't just a matter of principle: a just transition that's limited to moving men from oil rigs to wind turbines doesn't bring enough workers into the Green New Deal fight to win.

There are only around 50,000 coal miners working in the United States today and around 1.4 million oil and gas workers. That's a lot of people, and they all deserve to have good work after we abolish their industries. But they're not the entirety of the labor movement by a long shot.

By comparison, there are roughly 18 million health care workers, and 3.6 million teachers already doing low-carbon work. These workers are part of a labor movement that's fighting for good union jobs in connection to a larger expansion of public goods and services, while undertaking new kinds of organizing that reach beyond the workplace. And these workers are at the forefront of labor militancy. In 2018, the US Bureau of Labor Statistics reported twenty "major work stoppages" in which 485,000 workers went out on strike. Workers in education, health care, and social assistance accounted for over 90 percent of striking workers in 2018; workers in those sectors conducted half of all strikes between 2009 and 2018.[20]

That's still a ways off from the turmoil that produced the original New Deal. In the 1920s, there were over 500 strikes a year even at the low point in 1927. But the Red Scare of 1919–20 had been devastating to labor militants. No one would have guessed that fifteen years later, labor would be transforming national politics. By 1937, the

---

20 Bureau of Labor Statistics, "Work Stoppages Summary," bls.gov. February 8, 2019.

number of strikes had spiked to 3,500. When political momentum is growing, things can change fast. Even just a few years ago, a wave of militant teacher strikes was unimaginable.

Recent strikes also show how labor organizing can organize the working class more broadly. Bosses win when the storyline pits unions against the public good. So labor organizer Jane McAlevey argues that unions win when they do "whole-worker organizing"—organizing that sees workers as connected to broader communities, and that organizes those communities alongside them.[21] And when unions fight and win this way, the whole community wins, too, building the foundations for further gains.

The United Teachers of Los Angeles have organized in the workplace and the community for over a decade, on a model known as bargaining for the common good. When teachers went out in the streets early in 2019, the community went out with them. They won better contracts, more teachers, more counselors, more nurses. They created an immigrant defense fund. They won a commitment to more green spaces and more gardens. They won, that is, a lot of things we imagine as part of a radical Green New Deal.

Strikes teach people how to fight and win. When workers organize their workplaces, they're ready for other

21   Jane McAlevey with Bob Ostertag, *Raising Expectations (And Raising Hell): My Decade Fighting in the Labor Movement* (Verso 2012).

political battles. In 2019, seven years after the Chicago Teachers' Union strike, six socialists were elected to the Chicago City Council. The current wave of teachers' strikes will surely seed new political movements, too. In West Virginia and Louisiana, teachers have fought to make the fossil fuel industry pay more in taxes to fund schools and teachers' salaries: teachers in West Virginia echo the struggles of coal miners before them. Public sector workers could do the same with technology in the Bay Area and finance in New York.

When teachers go on strike, they don't stop capitalists from making money—but they do have a direct line to the state. Many workers in health care and education are public employees, and even private institutions in those sectors rely on state funding. So those workers are well positioned to organize alongside movements pushing for the expansion of social services. The Amalgamated Transit Union has backed the Green New Deal, calling for "public transit, free for all, arriving on time, available around the clock, and completely powered by the wind, sun, and seas."[22]

Workers in health care have supported climate action because the people they serve are vulnerable to environmental harm and climate breakdown. National Nurses United, for example, argues that "bold action is needed to address the catastrophic health impacts of global warming,

---

22   ATU Media Center, "Can Public Transit Help Save the Planet," atu.org.

and the associated extreme weather conditions such as widespread drought, wildfires, and flooding all over the world."[23] That kind of solidarity can extend beyond local communities: Hector Figueroa, the late president of Service Employees International Union 32BJ, which endorsed the Green New Deal early on, explained that many union members have family in the Global South, where climate change is likely to have major effects. More generally, the workers of the world could be a source of power for climate action in the United States. Immigrants constitute a sixth of the American workforce; including undocumented workers, the number is even higher. Many have direct connections to people living in countries likely to be hit hard by climate change. And historically, it was the multiracial, multi-ethnic proletariat that formed the basis of militant CIO union power.

Today, the Green New Deal's most prominent labor supporter is Sara Nelson, president of the Association of Flight Attendants. She rose to prominence when flight attendants, along with federal air traffic controllers, called out sick a month into the 2018–19 government shutdown, forcing Republicans to back down from demands for a border wall. Nelson has argued that "our federal government must spearhead a national mobilization that … harnesses American ingenuity, creates millions of

---

23   National Nurses United, "Environmental and Climate Justice," nationalnursesunited.org.

well-paying union jobs, and saves the planet for our children."[24] She's also reminded climate activists to take workers' concerns seriously.

Much work is required to bring other sectors on board—extractive sector workers as well as the building trades. Paradoxically, many unions whose workers would likely benefit most directly from a Green New Deal have remained skeptical, on the premise that a job in the hand is worth two promises from a politician.

The building trades have long been among the most conservative forces in the American labor movement—but they have much to gain from the kinds of large-scale public works and infrastructure projects that a Green New Deal would undertake. Building trades unions already work on renewables projects and could organize for higher wages in the green sector. And construction workers, like others who work outdoors, are on the frontlines of rising temperatures.

There are other openings. Coal companies that have gone bankrupt are stiffing workers on pensions and health care; climate activists can show solidarity with miners by backing their fights to preserve their benefits. When United Steelworkers members struck at oil refineries around the country in 2015, they were joined by environmental justice groups and nurses' unions in the Bay Area, where a

---

24 Sara Nelson, "Flight Attendants Know the Real Job Killer Isn't the Green New Deal. It's Climate Change," vox.com, April 17, 2019.

refinery explosion in the multiracial working-class city of Richmond had recently sickened 15,000 people.

We need to imagine many more such coalitions: bargaining for the common good isn't just for public sector workers. Imagine a coalition of construction workers' unions and housing movements rallied around a commitment to building dense, no-carbon public housing on a mass scale, accessible to all. Imagine health care workers organizing alongside day laborers affected by heat waves, or fast food and meatpacking workers organizing alongside animal rights activists against the treatment of both human and animal lives as disposable. Imagine transit workers shutting down a major city for a day in conjunction with groups organizing for free transit, or sanitation workers refusing to pick up the trash until cities commit to building recycling and compost facilities and hiring workers to staff them, backed by communities affected by landfill contamination. We don't have these movements yet—but it's time to start building.

Unionizing green jobs is crucial for making them good jobs. The renewables industry currently has a low unionization rate—but that presents an opportunity for union growth. Public sector investment can set the standard for good work. More robust labor protections will also help. The Wagner Act—also known as the National Labor Relations Act—was the labor standard of the New Deal. To date, it offers the most sweeping set of labor protections American workers have ever had. But its

shortcomings are well known. Its protections against the
boss, restricted by the Taft-Hartley Act a little over a
decade after its passage, are far too weak. And today,
bosses are richer and stronger than ever.

We're long overdue for an update—one that institutes
card check, making it easier to form a union; forcefully
sanctions bosses who try to dissuade organizing; protects
workers' rights to picket and disrupt; regulates labor
markets above the level of the firm; recognizes the vast
number of workers who land in the gray areas of labor law,
from home health aides to farmworkers; and decriminal-
izes areas that land firmly outside of it, like sex work.

Labor organizers themselves have often argued that
being alive in the sunshine is key to the good life. In 1912,
Pauline Newman, the socialist organizer of the International
Ladies Garment Workers Union, wrote an editorial about
what workers stood to gain from working less.

> What a glorious time is Spring! Despair vanishes,
> gloom is forgotten … How would you like to run about
> the recently awakened country rather than sit at the
> machine! Oh, how you would like to drink in the pure
> air and be warmed by the sunshine! How you would
> like to roam about in the fields, dreaming and admiring
> the beauty of Nature![25]

---

25   Pauline M. Newman, "The Long Working Day and Spring," *Life
and Labor* 2, January 1, 1912.

Instead of roaming the fields, though, garment workers sat in the factory for ten hours a day. It could be otherwise, Newman insisted: "A six-hour day in Spring! What a delight it would be to leave the factory, the mill, the department store, while the sun is still shining!" If—and only if—workers stood together in the union, they could win the most precious thing of all: their time. "Spring is here, everything is alive, everything is awakening," Newman exclaimed. "Come, girls, wake up and demand your own!"

We, too, can have our time in the sunshine. But we, too, will have to fight for it.

3
REBUILDING THE WORLD

In 1933, the Tennessee Valley Authority (TVA) hired Hungarian immigrant architect Roland Wank to design housing for workers and people displaced by the construction of the Norris Dam. The TVA would provide cheap, renewable power in a poor part of the country neglected by a price-gouging private utility.

Wank had long experience with workers' housing in urban contexts. On the Lower East Side, he had designed the Amalgamated Dwelling, a cooperative complex for garment workers, built as an homage to Vienna's great socialist housing complex, the Karl Marx Hof. Exemplifying the interwar Left's urban vision, the Amalgamated—which still stands—included a vast courtyard, library, small stage, and roof decks for residents to play music and dance into the night.

In Tennessee, the Norris Dam's project lead gave Wank the dam designs and asked for his feedback. Wank had no experience with energy infrastructure. Two weeks later, he came back with a wholly different design. He built an elegant, charismatic structure, characterized by the dam's simple, diagonal slant. It was both monumental and intimate, an accessible offering to the region's inhabitants. There were viewing plazas on each of the dam's sides and an approach road that gave incoming visitors a sudden, dramatic view of the infrastructure. In the words of one gushing critic, as visitors drove up, the dam rose from behind the "wooded flank of a mountainside" like "the Acropolis."[1]

Wank became the chief architect of the TVA, where he designed several celebrated dams and innovative workers' housing. And he helped organize the Rural Electrification Administration, which established energy cooperatives that brought affordable energy to rural America for the first time. They still serve over 40 million people.

Wank's career in urban housing and rural electricity illuminates the connections between disparate parts of the physical world: what today we'd call the "built environment." That phrase captures the encompassing nature of our physical systems, while reminding us that they are literally *built*—subject to technological and cultural forces, and to political and artistic choices. We examine them here,

---

1   Frederick Gutheim, "Roland Wank, 1898–1970," *Architecture Forum* 133, 1970, p. 59.

starting with energy and then moving to housing, transit, and public recreation.

We outline how a radical Green New Deal could build landscapes of no-carbon splendor in and beyond cities. Our overarching goal is limiting energy use while simultaneously improving quality of life. Reducing demand shrinks the amount of minerals we have to claw out of the earth's crust. And the less total clean energy we have to produce, the faster we reach zero carbon. We get there by treating the whole energy system as a public good, not a private amenity—connecting dots between photons and transit, electrons and housing, photovoltaic panels and sunbathing. By prioritizing public splendor, we dance more lightly on the earth. The political upshot: a holistic, systems approach that connects struggles on a wide range of issues, building broader and more durable movements. As suggested in the Introduction, responding to crisis would provide political and fiscal stimulus to get started. Now is the time to debate visions for what we might achieve when we get the chance—and start laying the groundwork.

Meeting Sun and Wind Where They're At

Energy dominates climate discussions. At present, it's the cause of most carbon pollution. About four tenths of US energy is currently consumed in the form of electricity, mostly produced from fossil fuels. The rest mainly comes from their direct combustion, as in gas-powered cars or coal-fired steel mills.[2] The easiest way to decarbonize energy is to electrify (almost) everything that now runs on fossil fuels, from stovetop cooking to bus travel, so that it can run on renewable energy instead, while also increasing efficiency and building clean power supply. Electrifying energy saves some power automatically: over half the energy produced by burning coal, oil, and gas is lost as waste heat.[3] Still, to meet our projected energy needs, we'll need to decarbonize all that electricity production while roughly doubling how much we make. Hard work! (Again: we need to curb demand.)

To do that, we need public institutions, public ownership, and democratic controls—both to make change quickly enough and to increase accountability. For better or worse, some of the key technical details are too political to leave to the wonks.

These days, public debate about energy turns on the narrow question of how quickly and cheaply we can build wind turbines and solar panels. But that's the easy part. Wind and solar costs are plunging so fast that in much of the country, it's more expensive to keep burning coal than to close those coal plants *and* absorb lost revenue *and* build

2 "US Primary Energy Consumption by Source and Sector, 2017," eia.gov, eia.gov/energyexplained/images/charts/consumption-by-source-and-sector.png.

3 Lawrence Livermore National Laboratory, "Energy Flow Charts," flowcharts.llnl.gov/commodities/energy.

new wind and solar. The hard part is massively accelerating deployment, integrating the new technology, and shutting down the fossil industry at breakneck pace. The other great challenge—and this chapter's focus—is shaping the new energy system itself: where we build renewable sources, how we move clean energy, and how (much) we use it.

To think about the conventional energy system, it's best to simplify with metaphors. Picture two webs. First, there's a horizontal one that spreads across space, connecting nodes all across the country. Second, there are vertical webs that tumble down like beanstalks from power plants to end-users: buildings, factories, and electric vehicles.

In the traditional fossil system we're leaving behind, these webs work simply. An extensive horizontal grid is ideal. The larger the area, the more easily you can ramp up production in power plant A if power plant B has a problem. There's no need for an epic web, though, because coal, gas, nuclear, and hydro power are pretty reliable. Indeed, the United States still lacks a fully connected grid running coast to coast.[4]

In vertical terms, the power plants shoot energy downward, through the grid, to apartments, offices, and

---

4 David Roberts, "We've Been Talking About a National Grid for Years. It Might Be Time to Do It," vox.com, August 3, 2018. This article also inspired our use of the vertical and horizontal metaphors.

factories. The supply has to be carefully calibrated to meet demand. The challenge here is simply to ramp power plants up or down based on the energy use below.

In a renewables-dominated system, there are two big differences. First, the new power sources are intermittent. The sun doesn't always shine and the wind doesn't always blow, though over a vast country, one or both are happening somewhere. The more extensive your grid, the more easily you can move power to where it's needed.

Second, more energy now also flows *up* to the grid from below: rooftop solar panels, home and vehicle batteries, and other so-called "distributed energy resources" send electricity up the same wires that it comes down from solar farms, wind turbines, and dams and nuclear plants. When they're plugged in, electric car batteries can pull power down—or send it back up. (To reach carbon zero fast, we'll keep many dams and nuclear plants online a while longer, as long as they're safe.)

Getting to the smooth, no-carbon grid will be fiendishly technical—and intensely political. Done right, adjusting our energy system to take advantage of renewable sources could make our lives easier, and even more lovely.

Big, Clean, Public: A National, Democratic Grid

Some of that future already feels familiar. Picture milk-white turbine blades rotating slowly on the horizon of Vermont's Green Mountains or Montana's Black Hills.

Imagine dark blue solar panels on rooftops and clustered in fields, nestled amid pollinator-friendly flowers, repopulating the land with bees. Some of these energy fields will be more industrial, especially when they're far from population centers. We can picture those, too. And we've all seen the unionized workers who build, set up, and maintain this clean energy grinning on green jobs pamphlets.

But public discussions of clean energy often neglect the complementary work of completing a national web of high-voltage transmission lines. Crossing ocean-to-ocean, the expanded grid would use no-carbon power to cool and heat homes, warm water for showers, move trains and buses, and power factories. Especially in cities, we tend to ignore the political stakes of building this new web and how it will affect the environments of tens of millions of people beyond city limits.

The most efficient system for a big country like the United States is a sprawling, fully integrated grid, with microgrids nested into the system—able to detach but normally plugged in. When clouds soften the California sun, wind from Texas can charge Los Angeles's buses; when the Georgia sun sets, offshore winds on the eastern seaboard could power Atlanta's streetlights.

We need more than just wind and solar. Our new grid would also move energy from so-called "firm" no-carbon energy resources that backstop turbines and panels, like familiar hydro, plus new, emerging options like expanded geothermal and hydrogen stored in salt caves. More research funding could accelerate our use of these firm resources, cutting the amount of new wind and solar we'd need by roughly a quarter. We'd also move energy from giant landscape batteries that store up excess energy from sunny and windy seasons. Pumped hydro systems are the most common: excess clean energy pumps water uphill; when the power is needed, the water is released, turning turbines as it flows back down. In some areas, you can even use excess energy to compress air in giant caves, pressing it together like an invisible spring. Then ease up on the spring to release the energy back into the system.

The continental grid, new firm resources, and landscape batteries sound big. They are. This isn't the entirely decentralized vision of climate advocates of the Left or Right, who see solar panels and batteries as a chance for total local autonomy, leaving behind an archaic centralized system. But a continental system is by far the most efficient way to provide reliable, affordable, clean power to everyone.

On closer inspection, libertarian dreams of clean energy islands are insular and ultimately discriminatory. They offer nothing to communities that are poor, dense, or badly located for sun and wind, and that can't afford to install tons of solar panels and vast amounts of battery storage. Mostly, so-called "grid defection" is an option for affluent enclaves: resource-intensive solar separatism for the rich and the geographically lucky. Such solar separatism might seem novel—at root, it's just a new version of private schools and health care.

What's more, the big grid isn't the opposite of local microgrids and resiliency: rooftop solar and other small, flexible resources will draw strength from the big public system and vice versa. Financially and physically, a big, clean, and public grid is the *very premise* of local safety and emergency autonomy. In turn, the more sophisticated local energy gets, the more smoothly the big grid will operate.

Picture two California towns near San Francisco, two dozen miles apart: Moneyville, a sprawling, wealthy suburb; and Peopleville, a mixed-income community with some large housing complexes. Imagine the latter connected by wires to San Francisco through a creaky electric grid, starved of funds because of rich communities' solar separatism. In this scenario, Moneyville has built its own energy supply and cut ties—physical and financial—with the regional grid after a spate of PG&E blackouts.

Now imagine a wildfire cutting Peopleville off from San Francisco, severing power lines and causing a blackout. Sure, a couple measly solar panels dumped by the impoverished utility might provide emergency power to a medical clinic.

But if Peopleville and Moneyville were also connected by wires, there would be no blackout. What's more, if Moneyville were paying into the same public utility as Peopleville, that utility could build Peopleville its own nested, emergency microgrid—namely, the capacity for temporary, essential-service energy autonomy in case of disaster. Even if all connected power lines went down, Peopleville could maintain light and safety while awaiting repairs. One day, no doubt, an unpredicted disaster will strike Moneyville, and Peopleville will return the favor.

The big grid won't work for everyone, everywhere. On an island like Puerto Rico, carbon-spewing diesel fuel is the current backup for grid malfunctioning. But it could be otherwise: Puerto Rico is blessed by sun and sea. Batteries could back up solar-powered microgrids complemented by wind. (Puerto Rico wants to explore offshore wind but is currently blocked by the colonial tilt of the Outer Continental Shelf Lands Act.)[5] And for remote rural cabins and villages countrywide, off-grid makes sense.

The Right warns that renewable energy will cover swaths of the country in wall-to-wall solar panels or dump ostensibly cancer-causing turbines in every rural backyard. These threats have no basis in fact. It is true, however, that building out renewables is a major infrastructure endeavor that will takes up space and change landscapes, though less than opponents claim. A recent MIT study projects that powering the entire country's electricity needs just with solar panels in 2050 would use as much

---

5   "Puerto Rico Congresswoman Introduces Bill to Study Offshore Wind Energy Potential," *Caribbean Business*, February 8, 2019, carribeanbusiness.com.

land as is currently devoted to coal mining, or three times the land area of all US golf courses.[6]

Still, shoving clean energy infrastructure down people's throats is a sure recipe for making them hate the Green New Deal. We need to focus on *how* renewables will be folded into landscapes—and here, the big issues are design, ownership, and speed.

Attention to local concerns is critical. Northern European models emphasize community input into the design of wind farms and frequent, co-operative ownership of renewable energy in order to build political support for clean energy development in rural areas, and institute genuine community control over local landscapes. In upstate New York in 2016, for example, a set of rural, utility-scale solar programs were blocked by towns and counties angered by developers' rushed location of new power generation. But once residents had their say and projects were modified accordingly, panels were going up within a year.[7] If public investment prioritizes building public support, it could change the game. We'll need more consultation, local benefits to affected communities, democratic ownership, and careful contextual design.

6   Reja Amatya et al., *The Future of Solar Energy: An Interdisciplinary MIT Study* (MIT 2015), energy.mit.edu/wp-content/uploads/2015/05/MITEI-The-Future-of-Solar-Energy.pdf, p. 130.

7   Steve Orr, "D&C Investigation: Big Solar Coming to NYS, Some Are Wary," *Democrat and Chronicle*, November 22, 2016.

Taking time to do local impact assessments and build community support means we may not always start with the biggest projects. While we design the big stuff carefully, we could immediately expand smaller scale renewables fastest, especially rooftop solar. Per unit of energy generated, it's less efficient than large installations. But it can save on transmission, create jobs, and provide resiliency during disasters. It brings the benefits of clean energy into people's everyday lives. Public agencies could finance no-cost installations on working- and middle-class homes and nonprofits and small businesses' roofs to speed adoption.

The other big spatial dilemma is transmission. The National Renewables Energy Lab finds that a 90 percent renewable energy grid will require doubling of the length of current energy transmission lines.[8] Proposed wind fields, solar arrays, and new transmission lines have all been slowed—and often blocked—by protests from the communities where new projects are planned. Greens sometimes decry opponents as selfish Not In My Backyard (NIMBY) types or victims of Koch Brothers propaganda. (In fairness, there's some of both.) But it's reasonable to be concerned about drastic changes to the place you live—especially when the costs are local and most benefits go to far-off urban consumers.

---

8   National Renewable Energy Laboratory, "Renewable Electricity Futures Study: Executive Summary," nrel.gov, 2012.

With deliberate democratic design, big renewable projects can be glorious. Imagine long meetings in schoolhouses where farmers, nurses, retirees, carpenters, steelworkers, architects, and technicians all talk through plans. We can recall Wank's efforts to beautify big energy amid the mass mobilization of the New Deal. And we learn from Northern Europe. On hillcrests, slopes, and crop-fields, turbines could be strung in elegant necklaces, following the Nordic tradition of artful, community-engaged wind landscape design. In farm and town country, solar panels can go up on homes' and barns' rooftops and carpet fields ill-suited to agriculture. Power lines can be buried.[9] It's expensive but worthwhile if it builds support for the grid we need. Landscape architects can also widen aboveground transmission corridors to add landscaped bike and hiking trails, giving humans and electrons parallel routes through woods and valleys.[10]

Automating Efficiency: The Sunflower Home

Sun and wind are free but capricious. Moving energy around the grid counteracts their caprice, but only to a point. Conservatives love this: the Right gloats that a

---

9   Julian Spector, "Siemens Buys Transmission Line to Take Iowa Wind to the Eastern Grid," GTM, March 12, 2019, greentechmedia.com.

10   Nicholas Pevzner, "The Green New Deal: Landscape, Architecture, and Public Imagination," *Landscape Architecture Magazine*, July 2019.

windless night will shut off your TV in the middle of the NBA finals.

That won't happen. What's more, using the latest technology, we can align more of our energy use with the elements' whims.

Sunny California sheds light on the challenge. During the day, the grid is swamped with solar energy. When people get home from work in the early evening, the sun is setting. People flick on lights, turn on the air conditioning, switch on the TV to catch the Warriors. Energy demand surges. Utilities burn natural gas to help meet demand. This is just a couple hours' worth of a broader problem: a predictable mismatch between peak energy demand and peak natural supply.

There's also seasonal variation. In California, the greatest amount of energy needed in a year is about 80 percent higher than the daily average. In many states, that ratio of annual peak to average demand is greater.[11] Overall, the United States has nearly twice the generating capacity it normally uses. With fossil fuels, you can always just keep more coal or gas on hand to burn when needed.

In a renewable system, you can't shove clouds out of the way to let the sun through. One way to meet peak demand is to overbuild, adding tons of extra solar panels and wind turbines, and a lot of storage. Sure, it'll keep the big game

---

11   Timothy Shear et al., "Peak-to-Average Electricity Demand Ratio Rising in New England and Many Other US Regions," US Energy Information Administration, February 18, 2014, eia.gov.

on TV. But systematic overcapacity, using up vehicle, home, and grid batteries, is costly and wasteful. Instead, algorithms can help create what we call sunflower homes—energy environments where electricity flow adjusts to follow the elements.

As the Princeton energy engineer Jesse Jenkins puts it, "When we increase demand flexibility, the need for battery storage plummets."[12] As we'll see in the next chapter, this is vital to avoid unnecessary mineral extraction in sensitive ecosystems. We increase flexibility by using so-called "smart" meters and appliances—smart because they tell utilities how and when we use energy, and because they allow systems to be remotely adjusted. Big tech companies are pioneering these systems, largely for affluent home-owners and businesses. In 2018, the Google Nest-dominated "smart home" market was worth $36 billion. Yet many people have resisted utilities' efforts to install smart meters in their homes. Some resist from the libertarian Right: they don't want the state in their thermostat. One Houston conservative notoriously used a pistol to chase away an installation technician.

Leftists have attacked smart meter deployment from private utilities for different reasons. Smart meters could be used to shut off electricity remotely, when people can't

---

12 Interview with Daniel Aldana Cohen, May 3, 2019. See also Nestor A. Sepulveda et al., "The Role of Firm Low-Carbon Electricity Resources in Deep Decarbonization of Power Generation," *Joule* 2, October 17, 2018.

afford utility bills. Let's be clear: in a radical Green New Deal there would be no shut-offs, because an affordable, comfortable home is a human right.

Our proposed sunflower homes would indeed allow utility algorithms to tamper with our home lives, switching off fridges, heat pumps, phone chargers, and other appliances for short blips to lower energy use at peak times. Instead of guilt-tripping individuals about turning off the lights or unplugging electronics, the smart grid would do it for us. Smart appliances would also run when clean energy is plentiful. Go to work, and let the computer decide when your super-efficient washer cleans your dishes.

Still, the smart meter resisters are on to something. This much system integration is frightening in an age of corporate and military surveillance. We don't want Google Nest or Amazon Alexa to "optimize" (and profit from) data on everything we do at home.

We need to replace the corporate platforms with public utilities that would use cutting-edge encryption to protect individuals' privacy from prying eyes. We would subject the open-source algorithms to the scrutiny of countless coders. This is an old-ish idea. As Shoshana Zuboff reports in *Surveillance Capitalism*, academics at Georgia Tech sketched a privacy-oriented data system called "Aware Home" almost two decades ago.[13]

13   Shoshana Zuboff, *The Age of Surveillance Capitalism: The Fight for a Human Future at the New Frontier of Power* (PublicAffairs 2019), p. 5.

The companies that supplanted them weren't more creative—just richer.

A radical Green New Deal would join coders' and consumers' backlash against the technology giants. We'd ally with the thriving open-source coding movement and politicized tech workers. Automating our energy use in a noncreepy way is one more reason for taking back control of our data. This could be part of a broader "platform socialism" organized through "digital commons" (to borrow phrases from British leftists) where the key physical and information systems that underlie our lives are brought under public control. This is an example of how thinking more expansively—and precisely, and accurately—about energy systems could further expand the political coalition for a radical Green New Deal.

Bringing thousands—maybe millions—of progressive tech workers into our movements will help ensure that every person benefits from the best technologies. Public control of algorithms will disinfect them with sunshine. And public procurement, finance, and California-style efficiency regulations would slash emissions and make the most advanced appliances available to all. People would trade in wheezing fridges and leaky gas stoves for slick, efficient upgrades—a bigger and better version of the Obama stimulus "cash for appliances" program.[14] Our

---

14 Elizabeth Shogren, "Cash for Appliances Program Takes Off," *NPR*, April 20, 2010, npr.org.

sunflower homes would be clean, safe, and comfortable. Everyone should have access to the best technology that society can offer.

Homes Guarantee: Upgrades and
Ten Million New Homes

A radical Green New Deal has to go even further, leaving the energy experts' comfort zone, where the housing market's structural inequalities are taken for granted. The real estate industry might disagree, but we see decent housing as a human right. And housing and carbon are tightly knotted. A Green New Deal for housing would drive decarbonization by guaranteeing homes for everyone.

Far from a massive add-on, a homes guarantee is the means by which we'll achieve many of the Green New Deal's goals of decarbonization, job creation, racial and economic justice, and higher quality of life. A multifamily building with sunny balconies might not evoke climate progress like a towering wind turbine. And yet homes are as much a part of our energy infrastructure as roads and power lines. They're also the private shelters where we sleep, eat, make love, and keep safe from the elements. We need as clear a demand for housing as we have for other major issues, like "Medicare for All" and "Free Public College."

A big bold ask will be the banner behind which the cavalries of public housing restoration, universal rent control, energy upgrades, anti-eviction support, and other new housing policies will gallop. Our banner: 10 million beautiful, public, no-carbon homes over the next 10 years, in cities, suburbs, reservations, and towns, in the most transit-rich and walkable areas.

Housing belongs at the Green New Deal's core for three reasons.

First, exploding costs have made housing inequality a driver of economic misery as important as unemployment and low wages. Nearly 20 million US households spend over one half of their income on housing, while a similar number pay between one third and one half.[15] Women, the young, and the racialized are disproportionately burdened. The country now faces a shortage of over 7 million affordable homes for poor and working families.[16] There isn't a single state in the country where someone working a full-time minimum wage job can afford a modest two-bedroom apartment.[17] Unaffordable housing can trap women suffering domestic violence, making it impossible for them to move out.

---

15 "Millions of Americans Spend Over 30 Percent of Income for Housing," Harvard Joint Center for Housing Studies, harvard-cga.maps. arcgis.com.

16 National Low Income Housing Coalition, "New Report Published Today: Shortage of 7 Million Apartments for the Nation's Lowest-Income Renters," nlihc.org, March 14, 2019.

17 Tracy Jan, "A Minimum-Wage Worker Can't Afford a 2-Bedroom Apartment Anywhere in the US," *Washington Post*, June, 13, 2018, washingtonpost.com.

And decades of racist housing policies have hardened the racial wealth gap, whereby the median white family has about $100,000 more than the average Black or brown family. That inequality extends to indoor energy use. In the middle Atlantic states, over half of Black households suffer "energy insecurity"—the inability to pay heating and cooling bills without major sacrifice.[18]

Housing inequalities of class and race are exacerbated in the desirable, dense, and job-rich places that we need to keep building up—or start building, as we increase public transit. Increased residential density, especially in suburbs and low-slung parts of cities, would cut emissions. But right now, densification plus transit often increases land values, pushing poor and working people out of newly walkable neighborhoods. This merely greenwashes the first steps to eco-apartheid, where only the white and affluent have access to the most pleasant, efficient spaces, while the burdens of pollution and decarbonization are piled on the backs of everyone else.

Cutting-edge quantitative research finds that, when residents of dense neighborhoods are wealthy, the footprint of their luxury consumption—from iPads to plane trips—overwhelms the carbon savings of walking to brunch. Per capita carbon footprints in the West Village

---

18   "Residential Energy Consumption Survey: Implications for Philadelphia," Philadelphia Energy Authority, March 12, 2018, philaenergy.org.

are two to three times higher than those of many comparably dense neighborhoods in the Bronx.

Dense, mixed-income, and working-class neighborhoods near public transit, anchored by public housing, are good to live in and have small carbon footprints. Objectively, the working class women of color who populate the housing movements that are fighting against gentrification and demanding *affordable* density are in fact low-carbon protagonists—whether they talk about climate or not. To make low-carbon neighborhoods ubiquitous, we would build out nonmarket housing and impose flexible, national rent controls. That would promote climate-friendly urban improvements—greening, new transit options, new and attractive buildings—that benefit the people who have fought for years to improve their under-invested communities without causing displacement.

Second, we'll need tens of millions of new homes overall. Sea level rise alone is projected to displace about 13 million Americans by the end of the century.[19] That doesn't factor in heat, humidity, drought, or inland flooding. As warming punishes countries in the Global South even more than in the United States, we should welcome far more immigrants. We need to plan for about 430 million Americans by 2100. American cities are full of vacant "investment" homes that should be repurposed. They're

---

19   Will Dunham, "Sea Level Rise Projected to Displace 13 Million in U.S. by 2100," *Reuters*, March 14, 2016.

also full of indecent, crumbling homes. Overall, we still need to increase affordable housing supply. The private market has been building well over one million units a year since 2015.[20] Our proposal is to displace much of that private construction with higher quality housing for a bigger group of people.

Third, a program of upgrading the buildings we have, and building new public housing to no-carbon standards, can be a lever for decarbonizing. The residential sector's energy use causes nearly one sixth of US carbon emissions. By 2050, residential efficiency upgrades could avoid emitting 550 million metric tons of carbon pollution per year— that's more than the combined 2016 emissions of all the power plants in California, Texas, New York, Florida, and Virginia.[21] Retrofitting buildings is a slog. We'd prioritize upgrading public and subsidized housing, following the lead of well-known projects in Boston, Toronto, Paris, and Bordeaux. Efficient new construction will make decarbonizing vastly easier and create hundreds of thousands of jobs.

The best accelerator of workers' skill-building and technological improvement? Smart public procurement. This is how we'll accelerate production and deployment of concrete that's low-carbon, then, no-carbon, and eventually carbon-absorbing. (Globally, cement accounts for 8

20   "United States Housing Starts," Trading Economics, tradingeconomics.com.

21   Khalil Shahyd, "Residential Energy Efficiency Is Largest Source of CO2 Reduction Potential," nrdc.org, October 5, 2017.

percent of carbon emissions. Public muscle can squelch that.)

The case for 10 million public, beautiful, mixed-income, no-carbon homes isn't a demand from nowhere. The People's Policy Project has proposed 10 million new public homes over the next ten years, People's Action is fighting for a Homes Guarantee including 12 million new public homes, and even the Clintonite Center for American Progress has proposed one million new public homes in five years. All advocate mixed-income complexes, democratizing governance, and experimenting with ownership models like limited-equity cooperatives and community land trusts.

Ten million units of social housing would cost less than the recent Trump tax cut. It would tackle racialized class inequality and would slash the profits of the real estate sector, with help from taxes to end land speculation. We're not shedding tears for exploitative landlords or Wall Street lenders. The New Deal's racist, public-private mortgage system—red-lining Black neighborhoods, helping only white families to buy homes—was one of its gravest failures. And as the historian and author Keeanga-Yamahtta Taylor has shown, subsequent public-private partnerships to increase Black and brown homeownership were really schemes of predatory equity that trapped households in spiralling debts.[22] It's only fitting that a Green New Deal

---

22 Keeanga-Yamahtta Taylor, *Race for Profit: How Banks and the Real Estate Industry Undermined Black Homeownership* (University of North Carolina Press 2019).

should attack the real estate industry and racial inequality head-on. And we'd be building on a wave of housing justice organizing that's already sweeping the country.

To be sure, building affordable housing in or near affluent, white neighborhoods is hard. But it can be done. In New Jersey, the country's densest state, the state forces every town to zone affirmatively for affordable housing thanks to the Mount Laurel doctrine, a legal precedent established in 1975. That legal victory was won, and has since been sustained, by multiracial, union-supported, progressive-backed campaigning. Federal action could improve housing fairness laws, and use legal and fiscal carrots and sticks to make local authorities eliminate single-family zoning and facilitate affordable housing. Many affluent homeowners will resist. But as we increasingly meet Americans' desperate housing needs, our power base of unions, racial and environmental justice groups and housing movements will grow. Contentious local battles will have the benefit of ensuring that new construction and planning is done deliberately, with sensitivity to local needs. And we'll be using new affordable housing to expand the Left's geographic reach beyond progressive strongholds. We'll build attractive clusters of homes in conservative rural areas, where the housing affordability crisis is often as bad as in big cities.

Good housing, after all, is the foundation for living well. There's a reason that Roland Wank's greatest housing project, the Lower East Side's Amalgamated Dwellings, was an homage to Vienna's Karl Marx Hof. That Austrian wonder is more important to twenty-first-century US climate politics than people might think.

The Karl Marx Hof still stands. It's a giant, shaded, peach-colored complex of 1,200 apartments, with rounded arches and fine stonework, surrounding broad lawns, fountains, and gardens. It remains the finest exemplar of the Red Vienna's (1919–34) world-best housing program, itself a far better model of social housing than the US New Deal's programs.[23] Vienna's leftist Social Democrats were first elected after World War I. They haven't lost a free election since. (They were, it's true, beaten by fascists in a civil war.) They saw housing construction as a lever for their broader projects of economic justice and human liberation.

In the 1920s, Red Vienna levied harsh real estate taxes that devastated the land market, making it cheap to buy land to build on. The tax was progressive: 0.5 percent of the city's properties provided 40 percent of the revenues. And the city raised a third of public housing funds from luxury taxes. A political poster from the period shows a muscular red fist swiping a bottle of champagne from an ice bucket, horrifying a bourgeois couple wearing tuxedo

---

23 Eve Blau, *The Architecture of Red Vienna, 1919–1934* (MIT Press 1989).

and gown. Vienna's Left seized the riches of the few to provide public luxuries for the many, taxing champagne, race horses, and servants to fund bricks, tile, and gardens for the working class.

As usual in Red Vienna, the complexes integrated sophisticated services. Karl Marx Hof had cultural facilities and a dental clinic. The social fabric woven into the housing developments connected socialist and labor housing commitments with the best ideas of a feminist movement that was born on the barricades of 1848, and a public health movement that quickly followed.

Vienna held design contests for public housing and the best architects competed. Because many trades workers were then unemployed, the homebuilding program hired thousands of craftsmen to do elaborate stonemasonry. Red Vienna's valorization of skilled blue-collar work yielded a stunning variety of gardens, stairwells, laundry facilities, and other common spaces. This didn't impress everyone. In 1934, the Brookings Institute reported that the beautiful housing was a waste of money—it would have been cheaper to build concrete shacks in the suburbs.

In fact, Red Vienna's social housing legacy kept improving with time. Today, roughly a third of Vienna's housing is still public, city-owned. Another third is limited-equity cooperatives, where the most innovative building designs now flourish. A final third is private, with good quality and low costs. Vienna's immigrant-dense, working-class neighborhoods, rich in public housing, vote in huge numbers against the arch-conservatives who are popular in rural Austria. The city has recently implemented free daycare for children aged zero to seven. Public transit costs a euro a day for a yearly pass.

Vienna is far from perfect. You can't have eco-socialism in one capitalist, European city. The Viennese Left hasn't figured out how to organize beyond city limits and is thus surrounded by an immensely conservative small-town Austria. Still, Vienna makes clear that lasting, creative, working class institutions that raise and spend money well really do make life better. And with an extraordinary transit system and dense housing, per capita carbon emissions are miniscule.

Today, American housing projects are unjustly stigmatized. It's also true that because US public housing was intended as a last resort for the destitute, it was often built on the cheap and always badly maintained, leading to demolitions and turning public housing into a symbol of urban decay. Vienna's radiant social housing incarnates its working class's socialist ideals; the United States' decaying public housing incarnates its ruling class's stingy racism.

A Green New Deal for the New York City Housing Authority, and other public housing systems, could raise their apartments to world-best standards of comfort and efficiency. Upgrades could also use batteries, common spaces—and where appropriate, combined heat-and-power systems—to make the complexes into neighborhood resiliency centers when disaster strikes. When building new social housing, we would include mixed-income populations to bring in more money and diversify the spaces, and use other financial tools developed in Red Vienna and Sweden to ensure that top-quality maintenance is always paid for. By contrast, most new affordable housing in the United States is now built through tax credits—an increasingly wasteful strategy that yields far too little housing, benefiting builders more than tenants. And those inefficient tax credits slow construction.

Diversity of governance and economic structures would also be key to a Green New Deal for Housing. Federal funding should allow groups to experiment with limited equity co-operatives and community land trusts, alongside housing built and governed by local authorities. In cities like Philadelphia and Baltimore, new units could be developed by buying up decrepit and abandoned properties, rehabbing them, and turning them into locally managed land trusts that restore community wealth. Public homes should be built in different shapes and sizes, depending on their urban, suburban, small-town, or reservation context. New buildings should blend into local communities. And aggressive oversight by auditors must stamp out opportunism and corruption: from Red Vienna to the New Deal, keeping public projects clean was key to building mass support. When public amenities are useful and attractive, people never let them go.

Move It

We also have to find better ways to get out of the house and move around. Gas-powered cars and SUVs are terrible for the climate. Of the 28 percent of US greenhouse gas emissions caused by transportation, over half comes from passenger vehicles alone.[24] But the best-known solutions are technocratic fantasies. Let's stretch the legs of some democratic alternatives.

As we detail in the next chapter, swapping each combustion engine car with an electric vehicle would cause a drastic increase of mining for lithium, cobalt, copper, and other minerals—far in excess of what we need and of what mining communities can bear. Plus, we don't want to live in the pathetic neoliberal green dream of anonymous shiny cities swarming with driverless Teslas. Nor are we impressed by the urbanists' chauvinist fantasy that we could all live in Manhattan-like cities, walking and biking everywhere with a tote bag loaded with ramps, smiling smugly at our green virtuosity.

In contrast, a radical Green New Deal for mobility can both embrace efficiency and emphasize public control, health, freedom, and mostly shared travel. We can be flexible and thoughtful in and beyond urban spaces.

The goal for cities and suburbs is a public transportation system that's free, and so good that most people will

---

24 "Fast Facts on Transportation Greenhouse Gas Emissions," US Environmental Protection Agency, June 2019, epa.gov.

support major restrictions on private cars (and ultimately a ban). Our workhorse would be the electric bus, operated by unionized drivers. Currently, over 99 percent of the world's 425,000 electric buses operate in China.[25] The United States should build and deploy more of these here. Over the lifespan of a typical city bus, electric vehicles are already cheaper than diesel. They're also more comfortable, nearly silent, and emit no exhaust. These are the buses you want to bike behind.

Detroit could be shedding SUV lines, its unionized workers building electric buses instead. Unions of public transit workers and automakers could band together for clean, collective mobility. We're inspired by the growth of electric rickshaws in China and India—if there's a way to integrate them in the United States, we support it. We also note that shared minivans and minibuses are ubiquitous in the Global South—and increasingly the North, like New York City's Flatbush dollar vans. We're inspired by all these variants of collective mobility.

So yes. We want more bullet trains, regional rail, subways, and streetcars. And we'll get them. Even trolleybuses, which use wires instead of batteries, are best longterm: cheaper and less resource-intensive. But new infrastructure takes time. Cities could immediately paint dedicated bus lanes for local and express service,

---

25 "Electric Bus, Main Fleets and Projects Around the World," Sustainable Bus, October 2, 2018, sustainable-bus.com.

practically for free. Under pressure from protestors, São Paulo created hundreds of kilometers of bus lanes in 2013–14 alone. And bus travel between cities is getting more popular, because it's cheap, chill, and increasingly online. Let's triple down. Make the buses electric, paint interstate bus priority lanes, add stations in suburbs to beat city traffic.

Buses can't do it all, though. Today, the so-called "last miles" of getting around are hardest, especially for those unable to walk, bike, or scoot. Countrywide, transit users resort to taxis or rideshares to plug gaps in patchy public systems. They also use them for groceries and errands. Private rideshares, like Uber Pool and Lyft Line, are aggressively crowding out public transit with pricey alternatives for the rich or desperate. We need to give transit agencies the levels of funding they need. We also have to recognize the threat of projects like Ford's ill-fated Chariot service, a San Francisco experiment in a larger minivan rideshare. These companies want to suck riders out of buses, trams, maybe even subways. They'll keep trying. What's the alternative to this eco-apartheid on wheels?

Imagine a public organization using the best algorithms to make minivans that could accommodate late-night lovers, strollers, wheelchairs, and walkers. Helsinki has tried this: its Kutsuplus was a rudimentary public, Uber Pool–like minivan that was hailed through the internet. It cost about 5 euros a ride, just a bit more than the 3 euro fare for normal transit. Kutsuplus built a devoted following but was canceled in 2016 amid austerity.[26] All the program needed was a major cash infusion to add vehicles and improve software.

A radical Green New Deal could invest in algorithms and app design. The Department of Transportation could provide capital funds to scale up fast; US cities and towns could integrate the flexible services into their networks. A Green New Kutsuplus (someone please come up with a better name) would be even more useful in suburbs and towns outside cities, where low density makes regular bus routes impractical, stranding working class people with costly rideshares as the only way to get to the job.

From Indigenous reservations to former Appalachian coal towns, local transit agencies or worker cooperatives could manage small fleets of nimble electric minivans, emancipating the freedom to move from the financial burdens—and ecological footprint—of car ownership. Yes, there would also be electric cars. The point is that there shouldn't *only* be cars.

The key for a radical Green New Deal is to reimagine density. We don't want a one-size-fits-all template of buildings clumped together. Rather, we're working for a density of no-carbon freedoms, supported by flexible infrastructures and a wide range of institutions. Different groups and places will get free in their own ways.

---

26 Olli Sulopuisto, "Why Helsinki's On-Demand Bus Service Failed," *City Lab*, March 7, 2016, citylab.com.

Playscapes

Decarbonizing is easier from a holistic perspective. Systems thinking and expanded ambition can build social and political support. We can organize around the no-carbon imperative to take back control of cutting-edge math, beautify our landscapes, ease our mobility, and guarantee lovely homes.

The argument has one last step. As we suggest throughout the book, one part of the ecological crisis stems from the excessive production and use of crappy things we don't really need. And as we outlined in the last chapter, guaranteed public services and shorter work weeks will give us more time. Where will we spend it? It can't be the mall. The New Deal precedent shows us the upshot of federal investment in shared spaces of leisure.

Back then, it was mainly an economic model: building spaces of leisure put people to work doing good things for themselves and neighbors, bettering life for people who weren't rich. Similar moves now would also be a climate model: sport, play, culture, reforestation, and ecosystem repair are activities consistent with decarbonization and protecting us from climate disasters. In most cases, they also involve landscapes of no-carbon play.

In the 1930s, New Deal reformers worried that with the end of prohibition and the shortened, forty-hour work week, workers would use their newfound time to turn the country into a giant saloon, dissipating themselves in whiskey, poker, and prostitution. The public recreation movement saw improvements to the built environment as a healthier way to close the "leisure gap" between workers' free time and available amenities. The paranoia was silly. The preventative measures were glorious.

New Deal agencies invested more in public recreation than almost any other form of infrastructure, rivaling sewer systems and educational facilities for total dollar outlays. It paid off. Cities like Philadelphia expanded massive greenspaces like the Wissahickon Valley Park, which is still wondrous. New York tripled its stock of playgrounds, San Francisco doubled its number of parks. The New Deal also helped nationalize the country's beaches and funded spectacular beachfronts, like Robert Moses's Orchard Beach in the Bronx, with a colonnade, restaurant, promenade, picnic and games area, and tennis and handball courts. Moses also built ten magnificent public swimming pools in New York City, still teeming with swimmers today. In New York alone, FDR's government funded a workforce of 1,800 designers, draughtsmen, and engineers in Moses's agency, all devoted to public leisure. Big cities like Chicago, Milwaukee, and San Francisco (and smaller ones like Raleigh, North Carolina; Kearney, Nebraska; and Stearns, Kentucky) all gained pools and bathhouses.[27]

---

27   Phoebe Cutler, *The Public Landscape of the New Deal* (Yale University Press 1985).

The 1930s public recreation also movement spread outside cities: the Civilian Conservation Corps built recreational facilities and FDR multiplied the country's national parks. Even the New Deal's energy system became a tourist trap. Nearly four and a half million people visited TVA dams in their first decade. It might be hard to get millions to gape at wind farms and fields of solar panels, however carefully they're designed. But the massive conservation programs, ecosystem restoration, and rewilding that a Green New Deal calls for won't be for carbon reductions alone. We can imagine vacationers slipping out of cities on sleek electric buses and trains to camp by lakes and lounge on beaches. Others will choose hardier stuff: hiking through lush foothills, bird-watching in thickened marshes and wetlands, kayaking through frothing rivers. Kids and grown-ups can still pick apples, pumpkins, and berries— only now, they'll also be learning sophisticated new low-carbon techniques for growing good food, the new sustainable farm system that everyone wants. As the landscape architect Billy Fleming has argued, a Green New Deal could once again put the greatest talents of the design profession to public use.[28]

We can also use a radical Green New Deal to revitalize one of our greatest collective pastimes: sports. Today, public funds are siphoned into giant energy-sucking

---

28   Billy Fleming, "Design and the Green New Deal," *Places*, April, 2019, places journal.org.

stadiums for a corporate culture that hijacks kids' enthusiasm, overpays owners and megastars, and shreds the lives
of gifted athletes who don't make it to the top. Meanwhile,
parents spend hours and small fortunes getting their kids
to soccer fields or swimming pools, while teens shoot
hoops on shoddy basketball courts. A radical Green New
Deal would make easy access to quality sports facilities a
right for everyone.

Building Freedom

Rebuilding the world for climate justice is about transforming how we work and live: the stone, glass, wood, and
steel that we shape with our hands to protect us from the
elements—and bind us to their beauty. The politics of
climate change and the transformation of the built environment are the same damn thing.

Those politics must be anti-racist to the bone. Today,
our spaces are deeply segregated—many thanks to the
New Deal, when Northern liberals supportive of FDR cut
deals with white supremacist Southern democrats exclud-
ing Black people from programs that bettered lives. The
Norris Dam housing that Roland Wank built for dam
workers and displaced people excluded Black Americans—
even though it was located in the heavily Black South.
Dams on the Columbia River in the country's Northwest,
meanwhile, severely disrupted Indigenous lifeways. The
New Deal cultural front did better, empowering people of

color to tell their own stories in a panoply of art forms. We can do better still.

A radical Green New Deal would invest in Indigenous nations, communities of color, and working-class groups in ways that gives them power over their built environment. Funding cooperatives and land trusts for housing, energy, and transit systems is just one example of the diversity of models we want to foster through investment and experiment. The environmental justice communities that have borne the brunt of pollution should be first in line for clean electric buses, housing upgrades, new street trees, and new swimming pools. Targeted investment in the groups and places that have suffered most isn't only compensation—it's an effective, efficient lever for decarbonizing and liberating at once.

In the decades of neoliberal despair, it has often felt impossible to imagine that the physical world was actually responsive to political projects, that infrastructure could be a medium for radical, fast-moving action steered by democratic publics. These days, change to infrastructure is carceral, like the construction of endless new prisons. Or in slightly friendlier guises, it comes with fees: apps to pay for parking, toll roads, higher fares for substandard subway service. Infrastructure as crumbling, immovable burden.

No More. When we reinvent state institutions and invest democratically, we'll reshape our built environment in ways that decarbonize, make us safer, and abolish inequalities. There will be more than electric wires linking

beautiful public housing, speedy trains, and verdant landscapes of public, renewable power. These projects will be
linked by an irresistible dream: ordinary people seizing
control of their place in the world. Stopping the climate
emergency will be our chance to build glorious communal
luxuries—planted tree by tree, strung light by light,
sculpted stone by stone.

4
RECHARGING INTERNATIONALISM

In the future we just described, we'd live in fully electrified affordable housing, reduce our energy demand with democratic algorithms, and use free no-carbon transit to travel for (less) work and (more) leisure, enjoying lovely parks, theaters, and landscapes. We'll need muscular social movements and insurgent policymakers to make this happen.

We'll also need minerals extracted from the earth. Like the fossil energy system, renewable energy requires natural resources from around the world: cobalt, copper, lithium, nickel, and a host of rare earth minerals used to produce solar panels, wind turbines, battery storage, and electric vehicles. But their extraction and refinement can cause intense social and environmental harm—costs that don't show up on companies' bottom lines. And as clean-tech capitalists increasingly worry about securing these crucial inputs, their extractive frontiers are emerging as new battlefields in trade wars and global power politics.

If capitalists undertake yet another race to the bottom, the global economy of renewable energy could echo the violence and degradations of fossil capital while also slowing global decarbonization. A Green New Deal could both help prevent a brutally exploitative expansion of mining and begin to construct a global energy economy that's more sustainable and more just.

The United States has a crucial role to play. Today, it's the greatest obstacle to global climate justice. It's one of the world's top carbon emitters, both overall and per capita; and it's growing its fossil fuel exports faster than any other country. In the early decades of the twenty-first century, the United States blocked global climate agreements while shoving through global trade deals, helping write the rules of trade to favor corporate power above all else. Here, we argue that the way forward on global climate action isn't just through more international negotiations—it also requires tackling the places where the institutions of the global economy meet the climate crisis.

The domestic legislation and mobilization we've described so far would make a huge difference to global climate politics. But the boundaries of the nation-state can't be the boundaries of our political imagination. For a Green New Deal to confront the planetary dimensions of climate change, it needs to be internationalist in scope, forging new solidarities and partnerships with social movements and governments around the world. That will involve diplomacy between states and the renegotiation of trade rules, as well as international coordination by social movements, to force governments and companies to comply with democratic values.

But meetings and summits alone aren't enough to change economic structures. We also have to engage directly with the supply chains where the essential minerals of the renewable energy sector are mined, manufactured, and eventually deployed. The rapid and comprehensive energy transition we've laid out is already plunging us into the ethical, economic, and ecological challenges that come with a renewable energy economy.

We should always follow the money: Capitalists and their political accomplices are scrambling for dominance over resources and primacy in battery and electric vehicle manufacturing. As one analyst told the *Financial Times*, "whoever controls these supply chains controls industrial power in the twenty-first century."[1] We need to engage on this emergent terrain. The state and capitalist competition shaping these supply chains threatens to deepen the power imbalances that structure global affairs—but the flipside is that restructuring them offers

---

1 Ed Crooks, "US, Canada and Australia Join Forces to Tackle Metal Shortage Risk," *Financial Times*, June 11, 2019.

an opportunity to strengthen global cooperation around rapid, egalitarian decarbonization.

The Extractive Frontiers of 100 Percent Renewable

A renewable energy transition means less coal mining and less oil drilling. That's a good thing—we'd be doomed otherwise. But renewable energy requires increases in other forms of extraction. Some of this will mean the expansion of already enormous mining sectors, like copper, which is essential for electrical wiring. Other new mineral sectors will grow explosively, like lithium, cobalt, and a bevy of rare earth minerals.

Take rechargeable batteries, essential to electrifying transit and storing intermittent solar and wind power. Cobalt is a key ingredient. More than half the world's supply is currently sourced from the Democratic Republic of Congo, from hand-dug mines worked by children, with scant protection of workers' safety. Mining and refining of graphite, another battery component, causes air and water pollution in northeastern China. Nickel mines and smelters, mostly in Australia, Canada, Indonesia, the Philippines, and Russia, contaminate air and water. (The Philippines recently closed several mines because of their environmental and health impacts.) The batteries themselves are often manufactured in Chinese factories still powered by coal. And there's not much battery-recycling infrastructure, so at the end of their lives they become toxic waste.

Another element essential to rechargeable batteries is lithium. Chemical compounds of lithium—hydroxide and carbonate—are needed to make the energy-dense, light-weight, mobile batteries that power phones, laptops, cars, scooters, buses, and e-bikes, as well as the stationary batteries that store energy for renewable grids.

Lithium is too reactive and unstable to occur freely in nature. It either exists in compounds with other minerals in hard rock formations, or is found dissolved as an ion in brine—water with a high concentration of salt. Over half of the world's lithium reserves are contained in the brine wells below the surface of the Andean salt flats of Argentina, Bolivia, and Chile—high-altitude, rugged expanses of bright white and gray dotted with lagoons tinted red from the interaction of algae, sun, and wind.

How will the renewable transition affect the market for lithium? If we continue consuming energy as we do now, the global appetite will be voracious. Electric vehicles would be by far the biggest driver. Unless transportation patterns change, the vast majority of these vehicles will be individual passenger cars. The longer the cars' range, the bigger the batteries must be—and the more lithium (and cobalt, and nickel, and graphite) they would need.

According to the forecasts of the Institute for Sustainable Futures, if the world transitions to 100 percent renewable energy by 2050, lithium demand would amount to 280 percent of global *reserves* (the amount of a given mineral that's economically viable to extract) and 85 percent of global *resources* (the amount of that mineral that's technically feasible to extract).[2]

While demand for electric vehicles is projected to skyrocket, financing for new lithium projects is hard to come by—in part because it can take years before long-term investments pay off. Cathode, battery, and electric vehicle manufacturers are now scrambling to make deals that guarantee their access to the mineral. To wit: On April 5, 2019, Volkswagen AG partnered with Chinese lithium company Ganfeng to supply its electric vehicle line, which will launch seventy new models next year.[3] The partnership is part of what they call their "electric offensive" strategy. Ganfeng also has signed supply agreements with LG Chemicals, Tesla, and BMW.[4]

And it's not just corporations that are jockeying. The projected electric vehicle supply chain is becoming a new geopolitical battlefield. In May 2019, the Trump administration imposed a 25 percent tariff on a range of exports from China, including electric cars and parts, thus seriously limiting their penetration of US markets. President Xi Jinping threatened to restrict rare earth mineral exports,

2   Institute for Sustainable Futures, University of Technology, Sydney, *Responsible Minerals Sourcing for Renewable Energy*, Earthworks, April 17, 2019, earthworks.org.

3   "Volkswagen Secures Lithium Supplies," Volkswagen AG, April 4, 2019, volkswagen-newsroom.com.

4   Elena Mazneva, "China Moves Closer to Battery Domination with VW Lithium Deal," bloomberg.com, April 5, 2019.

which would hamper US manufacturing of electric vehicles, wind turbines, and solar panels.

China's grip on the lithium supply is just as important. Two-thirds of lithium batteries are produced in China, and Chinese companies are owners of, or investors in, most of the world's largest lithium projects, primarily in Chile or Australia.

The US government is countering with its own moves to secure access to lithium and other minerals, often speaking the bellicose language of national security and "energy dominance." In December 2017, Trump signed Executive Order 13817, establishing a "Federal Strategy to Ensure Secure and Reliable Supplies of Critical Minerals." In May 2019, Senators Lisa Murkowski (R-AK) and Joe Manchin (D-WV) introduced the American Mineral Security Act, which would streamline the permitting process for US-based lithium mines, easing environmental requirements for proposed brine projects across Southern California and Nevada.[5]

Lost in these struggles to control these newly valuable minerals is a simple fact: the less energy we use, the fewer such minerals we'll need. There's no iron (or copper, or lithium) law that states that the electric vehicle future must be dominated by cars. Buses and vans could transport just

5   Louis Sahagun, "A War Is Brewing over Lithium Mining at the Edge of Death Valley," *Los Angeles Times*, May 7, 2019; Ernest Scheyder, "US Senate Moves Forward on Plan to Develop Electric Vehicle Supply Chain," Reuters, May 14, 2019.

as many people just as effectively, while using a fraction as much lithium. As we argued in the previous chapter, a clean energy transition focused on shrinking energy demand would make it easier to hit zero carbon faster—and require less stuff to be dug out of the earth. That agenda pairs remarkably well with the demands of many communities on the frontlines of the new mineral extraction.

From Brine to Batteries

At present, about 30 percent of global lithium production originates in Chile. The country contains the world's largest reserves, with particularly profitable production conditions and several new projects in the exploration phase. What would a global renewable energy transition mean for the communities affected by the extraction of this newly essential mineral?

In a working class neighborhood of Santiago, Chile's capital, a mural proclaims a resource nationalist vision—"El litio para Chile" (lithium for Chile).[6] This demand draws on a long history in Latin America of claiming natural resources—in many cases oil—for the people.

A thousand miles away in northern Chile, the message is different. On the side of a road between the tourist hub

---

6   This section draws on fieldwork conducted by Thea Riofrancos in Chile, in spring and summer 2019.

of San Pedro and the Indigenous community of Toconao—one of eighteen Indigenous communities affected by lithium extraction—graffiti declares outright opposition to the mining of both lithium and copper.

In January 2018, communities blockaded that road to protest lithium extraction. The government had recently signed a contract with the multinational firm SQM, which tripled the firm's lithium extraction quota and extended its lease until 2030, even though the company owes the state millions in taxes and was caught illegally financing politicians and political parties. One of the world's largest lithium companies, SQM was a state-owned enterprise before Augusto Pinochet's dictatorship privatized it. Corporate exploitation is obviously bad, but it's not yet clear what the best alternative is.

The two positions signaled by these different graffiti—resource nationalism and frontline opposition—are distinct critiques of extraction from the Left. The first sees the problem as the domination of foreign capital; the second focuses on the destruction of ecosystems and livelihoods. The main difference between the two visions is how they answer core questions: who decides whether, and how much, to extract—and who benefits? A national majority, or local communities?

The potent contradiction at the heart of the energy transition is that switching from dirty oil, coal, and gas is necessary to avert climate chaos, but the extractive processes necessary to realize a world powered by wind

and sun entail their own devastating social and environmental consequences. The latter might not be as threatening to the global climate as carbon pollution. But should
the same communities exploited by 500 years of capitalist
and colonial violence be asked to bear the brunt of the
clean energy transition just to make the shift a tiny bit
easier for affluent suburbanites who love their SUVs?

This analysis drives the work of Sergio Cubillos, the
twenty-nine-year-old president of the Council of
Atacama Communities, the association of the eighteen
Indigenous communities that ring the Salar de Atacama
from which all of Chile's lithium exports are extracted.
In the Salar, Cubillos reports, lithium mining is suck-
ing up water, diminishing biodiversity, and violating
Indigenous territorial rights.

Cubillos argues that the Salar is in danger of becoming
a "hydrological sacrifice zone."[7] After Antarctica, the
region is the second-driest place on earth, and it is becoming drier by the minute thanks to both the lithium and
copper sectors. Across the Puna de Atacama, the high
Andean plateau traversing Chile, Argentina, and Bolivia,
lithium is extracted from brine underneath the salt flats.
Mining lithium essentially means mining water.

One lithium mining company alone removes brine at
a rate of 1,700 liters a second, transporting it to enormous evaporation ponds that let solar radiation do the

---

7   Interview with Thea Riofrancos, March 13, 2019.

work of further concentrating the valuable mineral. Removing brine from the Salar's complex watershed has the twofold effect of endangering species in this high-altitude wetland, such as the Andean flamingos that feed on brine shrimp, and of lowering the water table, reducing access to freshwater for Indigenous Atacameño communities. This is on top of the astounding rates of freshwater extraction required by nearby copper mines, which use water for processing. One of the two major copper companies holding water rights in the Salar extracts 1,800 liters of freshwater a second.

Both industries combined have created a grave hydrological imbalance. About 2,000 more liters per second of water leave the Salar than enter it. In this context, the council has declared its opposition to any new lithium extraction in the Salar de Atacama or in the dozens of other salt flats in northern Chile. As Cubillos puts it: "no more companies, no more extraction."

The council is engaged in various forms of legal action. The broader resistance is less polite. Atacameño communities are likely to continue the kinds of roadblocks and direct actions they've organized before. Meanwhile, the council's stance is already beginning to rattle investors: In February 2019, the Canadian-based Lico Energy pulled out of an exploration project in the Salar de Atacama because, in their words, "opposition from the local indigenous community is both immense and widespread and the Company does not see any way in which this project or property can be realistically explored or developed in the future by any corporate entity."[8]

Lithium extraction is also generating new forms of transnational movement-building. The recently founded Plurinational Observatory of Andean Salt Flats (*El observatorio plurinacional de salares andinos*) is stitching together a network of affected communities, environmental activists, and scientists in Argentina, Bolivia, and Chile. The observatory is a unique organizational form: plurinational both because it includes members from these three countries, and also in recognition of the multiple Indigenous nationalities within each of the countries' borders.

Co-founder Ramón Balcazar explains that instead of framing itself in negative terms as an "anti-lithium mining" organization, members choose to center a positive vision of the salt flats as complex and environmentally vulnerable socio-natural systems with cultural, scientific, and economic value. Through a series of activist convergences, beginning in Chile and then moving elsewhere in the Altiplano, the observatory hopes to promote ecologically sound, democratically articulated forms of development in the region.

Crucially, this is an internationalism from below. Members share information and strategies and may one

---

8 "Lico Energy Formally Drops the Purickuta Lithium Property Due to Unworkable Property Conditions," Lico Energy Metals Inc., February 18, 2019, Licoenergymetals.com.

day coordinate actions, traversing national boundaries and overcoming the logistical odds of organizing in underserved rural spaces. For hundreds of years, elites have fragmented the Indigenous peoples of the Andes and subjected them (as well as non-Indigenous *campesinos*) to rapacious forms of capitalist development: salt nitrate mining, copper mining, and now lithium mining. Now, the observatory, and the broader web of environmental and Indigenous organizations that it links together, offers a vision of a world in which ecosystems and territories are not sacrificed in the name of mitigating climate change. What they are fighting for is an alternative to what observatory member and social work professor Barbara Jerez calls "eco-coloniality": deepening extractivism in the name of preventing climate change.[9]

Alongside the Indigenous and environmental grievances are labor struggles. Miguel Soto worked for SQM before it was privatized, and he was imprisoned for a year after the 1973 coup. Through a glitch in the regime, he was able to return to his job after he was released and, despite widespread repression targeting leftists, worked as a union organizer. His union, Industrial Chile, organizes workers in metallurgy, textiles, manufacturing, forestry, and more; they began organizing workers in the lithium plants in 2000. Workers at the installation are fragmented across

9 Presentation, *Energías Verdes y Extractivismo en Salares*, Universidad de Chile, April 12, 2019.

thirty-three unions—a result of regressive Chilean labor law. And labor organizers work in a risky environment: SQM has fired numerous organizers as part of a concerted anti-union strategy.

In 2016, Soto, along with leaders from other trade union confederations and left-wing elected officials, launched the Lithium for Chile Movement. They declared Chile's export-led accumulation model exhausted: It has generated wealth for foreign companies and left poverty in its wake. They are calling for a suspension of any new agreements with lithium companies and for the nationalization of SQM, citing Salvador Allende's 1971 nationalization of copper. Their position resonates with the findings of a Lithium Commission convened in 2014 by Michelle Bachelet's center-left government: the commission unanimously recommended that the state enact its role as the "authentic owner of lithium resources," and nearly every member voted in favor of establishing a state-owned company to develop lithium projects.

The idea of nationalizing lithium is popular with many ordinary Chileans, though unlikely to happen imminently. While Indigenous and environmentalist activists often agree in theory that state ownership would be better than private capital, many are skeptical that a state enterprise would deviate from the extractivist logic of its private equivalents. CODELCO, the state-owned copper company, is not known for respecting Indigenous rights or ecosystems. This is a moment, many believe, to envision new paradigms of ownership, new ways of thinking about the energy transition, and a new system of socio-natural values.

On the ground, the politics of lithium extraction are complex and still evolving. But ultimately, these different grassroots demands aren't so incompatible. Under Chile's current right-wing government, nationalization doesn't seem to be on the near horizon. Meanwhile, some amount of lithium will be necessary for decarbonization. In this context, many activists in Chile, whether from Indigenous organizations or the labor movement, strive for more public control over extraction *and* strict limitations on mining in environmentally fragile areas. All of this would incentivize recycling existing lithium and pressure companies to develop less ecologically harmful forms of mining—such as extraction that doesn't require removing any brine from the Salar. We hope for greener mining techniques, but we shouldn't count on them.

Exactly how much is ultimately extracted will be shaped by many factors, especially firms' investment decisions, domestic regulations, and local protest. But national politics in the Global North are also decisive. Precisely how will we decarbonize? A world crawling with 300-mile range luxury electric sedans requires a lot more lithium, and mining, than a world flush with electric buses. And US trade policies can support environmental and labor standards—or undercut them.

The Green New Deal Beyond US Borders

Climate change is a global crisis. Preventing the worst outcome will require cooperation between countries to dramatically reduce emissions and transfer carbon-free technology; adapting to its effects will require action to protect the world's most vulnerable and to welcome migrants displaced by rising sea levels and droughts.

The Green New Deal, however, is typically framed as a domestic process taking place within US borders. Most conversations about the clean energy transition assume that the materials we need to zero out carbon are ready and waiting. But as we've seen, it's not so simple. How can we ensure that a clean energy transition is also a globally just one? And how can action in the United States help ensure decarbonization beyond our borders?

We argue that making global progress starts with the material chains that already link countries: networks of global trade, particularly as they pertain to the minerals necessary for the renewable energy transition. It's essential that rising energy consumption in huge middle-income countries like India and China be renewable as quickly as possible, and that renewable energy powers electricity for the billion people around the world without reliable access to it. For that to happen without devastating mining communities, the United States must reduce energy demand at home, set new labor and environmental standards in its trade policy, and share technological innovations rather than hoarding patents on them. This will also strengthen our hand in negotiations. Overall, if a US Green New Deal helps accelerate green investment worldwide, everything we do to prioritize equity and democracy across supply chains would bring broader benefits.

An element of this approach could be the "Geneva Principles for a Global Green New Deal." Authored by economists Kevin Gallagher and Richard Kozul-Wright, the principles make clear that the past four decades of neoliberal hegemony have exacerbated financial instability, inequality, and climate change. They call for a new global consensus centered on equitable development, multilateral cooperation, and rapid decarbonization. Efforts to draw attention to environmental damage and human rights violations are also cropping up among international NGOs.[10] Citing human rights abuses, Amnesty International has called on manufacturers to produce an "ethical battery" in the next five years.[11]

These efforts are laudable. But for an energy transition that is democratic and sustainable, we need more than the

---

10 Kevin P. Gallagher and Richard Kozul-Wright, "A New Multilateralism for Shared Prosperity: Geneva Principles for a Global Green New Deal," Global Development Policy Center, April 10, 2019, bu.edu.

11 "Amnesty Challenges Industry Leaders to Clean Up Their Batteries," Amnesty International, March 21, 2019, Amnesty.org.

interventions of professionalized NGOs and technocrats. We need to weave relations of solidarity that cut across the deep asymmetries that structure our globe. Labor unions and climate organizers around the world need to address the injustices of global supply chains in order to build a truly green economy.

The global stakes of energy transitions are high: Previous transitions to coal and oil deepened imperialism and racial capitalism. The advent of coal-powered factories in England dramatically expanded productive capacity—and intensified demand for raw materials, harvested and extracted by slaves and other forms of coerced labor from a vast network of colonies. And in the twentieth-century bid to switch industrial economies to oil, firms enlisted states and their militaries in a scramble for control across the Middle East and North Africa.

This long history of domination also engendered visions of a different planetary order. Between the 1955 Bandung Conference and the 1974 launch of the New International Economic Order (NIEO), there was a brief opening to create a more equal world. Across the Third World, much of it recently decolonized, governments aspired to escape the trap of extractive economies through a combination of state planning and coordination across the periphery. They took aim at what dependency theorists called "unequal exchange": countries that export raw materials and import value-added manufactured goods are always on the losing end of global trade.

But the aspiration of Third World solidarity was replaced by a competitive race to the bottom to offer globe-trotting capital the lowest wages and the least regulation. Neoliberal hegemony, consolidated after the end of the Cold War, reinforced the Global South's dependence on foreign investment. In some contexts, this took the form of low-wage manufacturing for export. In others, especially in Africa and South America, an extractive model of accumulation intensified around the export of primary commodities like oil, copper, sugar, diamonds, and timber, with multinational firms and local elites capturing most of the profits.

Capitalist extraction is still devastating local communities and ecosystems, causing territorial dispossession and environmental destruction—but directly affected communities are increasingly mobilizing in opposition. Resistance to lithium mining in South America foreshadows the coming social conflicts along the extractive frontiers of renewable energy.

We stand on the precipice of yet another energy revolution and at a fork in the road: solar-powered capitalism with a whole new set of opportunities for profit and pillage; or an internationalist Green New Deal, a historic opportunity to remake global power structures and our relationship to the natural world. We argue that the latter stands a much better chance of actually decarbonizing the planet.

Solidarity Across Supply Chains

Providence, Rhode Island is a long way from Chile's Atacama Desert. Yet a campaign there by the Democratic Socialists of America has developed a vision of energy democracy in the United States that is strikingly compatible with demands on the ground in the Atacama and fledgling efforts around the world to formulate principles for democratic, just supply chains for essential minerals. Here we adopt that campaign's principles, with minor modifications, to explore how visions of energy justice in the Global North and South can connect.

As we've discussed, private utility companies (and many of their mismanaged public counterparts) are an obstacle to a radical Green New Deal: they resist decarbonization; they have failed to upgrade their infrastructure to be resilient against extreme weather; and their profit model subjects millions of Americans to fuel poverty.[12] The solution to these interconnected problems is to decarbonize, decommodify, decolonize, and democratize the grid. Only when energy is governed by inclusive, collective decisions at the points of production, distribution, and consumption, all within planetary limits, will it truly serve human needs.

These principles have emerged in the context of local US grid struggles, but they speak to the energy system in

12   Adam Chandler, "Where the Poor Spend More than 10 Percent of Their Income on Energy," *Atlantic*, June 8, 2016, atlantic.com.

its totality. They'll no doubt need adapting to reflect campaigns for energy democracy around the world. Here we offer some suggestions.

We've already argued for democratizing utilities. In what follows, we argue that democratic control over energy is a global project. Our core premise is that nodes of the vast supply chains of the renewable transition are potential sites of solidarity across borders. We could organize around a new, fair, and sustainable trade regime, where working people at all points in the renewable energy supply chain have a voice in deciding how much to conserve, how much to extract, and how to improve communities' lives worldwide. How much of a given resource we use shouldn't depend only on how much of that resource physically exists. Most obviously, we shouldn't use all the world's fossil fuels just because they're there. But when it comes to other resources, we must similarly take into account the decisions made by workers and affected communities at every node of production and distribution. And we must acknowledge that the resources to build a low carbon world need to be shared among all countries. Everyone will be decarbonizing with similar tools. We should be flexible about how much clean energy infrastructure we ultimately build here in the United States. We're not the only ones making the decisions.

The most straightforward way to reduce the emissions and environmental destruction caused by the renewable energy transition is to reduce projected demand for the earth's resources. Fortunately, there's low-hanging fruit: Our current consumption comes with a lot of waste. The electronics industry, for example, is premised on planned obsolescence, pushing people to buy new gadgets every year and making it hard to repair broken ones. We can follow Sweden and other countries in reclaiming the right to repair our objects, setting new standards for everything from smart phones to washing machines to make them easier to fix instead of throwing broken things away.

There's also progress to make in recycling battery materials (like cobalt and lithium) as well as reusing electric vehicle batteries in second-life applications, such as the less-intensive work of grid storage. Extraction should be held to stringent environmental regulations, and, in some cases, subjected to moratoria pending holistic impact assessments and improved mining techniques.

More broadly, across the Global North we need to change how we consume. As we've argued, attempting to minimize environmental impact one consumer choice at a time is a dead end. The *collective* changes in consumption we've outlined are essential.

Reducing resource demand in the Global North will also transform the power relations that structure the global economy. It's the responsibility of the Global North to ensure that the energy transition at the core of the Green New Deal doesn't replicate neocolonial patterns of dispossession and contamination. Dismantling over 500 years of colonial structures is a formidable task—but a major economic and energy transition is a good place to start. In the United States, we can fight to force our government and transnational corporations to respect the rights of workers in cobalt, copper, lithium, and other resource sectors. Decolonizing renewable energy also means respecting the rights of local and national publics to govern resources, honoring Indigenous rights as they're codified in international conventions, and involving Indigenous peoples in the ownership and governance of mining projects.

Those may sound like abstract principles. But US trade policy is one of the major forces shaping how commodities travel the world and under what conditions. A radical Green New Deal would need to overhaul it.

Currently, trade rules and agreements are written by and for the 1 percent. They protect capital's mobility and investors' profits and undermine the power of democratic majorities to prioritize labor rights, ecosystem integrity, and equitable economic development. Restructuring this global architecture, which is embedded in everything from investor arbitration clauses to intellectual property rights, is daunting. But there was nothing inevitable about the victory of the neoliberal project to protect markets from democracy. And this moment of heightened political turbulence presents an opportunity to reimagine the world freed from the imperatives of market fetishism. Across the Atlantic, the deceptively named "free" trade regime has come under attack—most prominently from the revanchist right-wing. The Left needs its own vision for trade. The globally dispersed supply chains of the renewable transition are an important place to start proposing policies that promote the interests of the 99 percent and the planet, rather than those of corporations and financiers.

Reactionary right-wing populists in Europe and the United States have tapped into long-simmering discontent with the free trade projects of the 1990s: the European Union, North American Free Trade Agreement, and above all the World Trade Organization. Right-wing populists promise to protect labor from competition with lower wage workers in the Global South and to restrict immigration. But nativism is a tool to paper over domestic class conflict. Workers share interests across national boundaries, and dividing the working class only weakens its bargaining position against globe-trotting capital. A Left trade policy would lift environmental and labor standards for workers and their communities wherever American companies, or their suppliers, do business.

The trade policy of a radical Green New Deal could end the race to the bottom logic of global capitalism. Instead, we would race to the top for labor and environmental standards, including "ratcheting mechanisms" to improve standards over time. We would also reverse the logic of trade negotiations: progressive state officials would negotiate so that labor, human rights, and environmental clauses are agreed upon *before* anything else is addressed, instead of being tacked on as an afterthought (if at all). Deals would require free, prior, and informed consent on the part of Indigenous communities located at the sites of extraction. One of the biggest challenges in holding US corporations accountable for the practices along their broader supply chains is enforcement in the absence of a global state. Historian Erik Loomis argues that labor activists should use a domestic law, the Alien Tort Claims Act, to try US firms for rights violations beyond US borders; Indigenous and environmental activists could, too.[13]

We would also prioritize mechanisms to transfer funds and technologies to the countries of the Global South to help them cut carbon emissions and adapt to climate change. Strong international intellectual property rights are a key part of the neoliberal project. Addressing them will be an important part of undoing it. Pharmaceutical industry influence on trade policy in the 1980s, for example, allowed US-based corporations to monopolize life-saving drugs like HIV/AIDS antiretrovirals, making them unaffordable for most in the Global South. It is essential that we avoid a repeat for planet- and life-saving clean technology—the tighter the grip of capital on clean technology is, the harder it will be for the world to decarbonize.

In the case of rechargeable batteries, we could require US-based lithium companies to adopt technology that doesn't damage sensitive watersheds in the Atacama Desert

13   Erik Loomis, "A Left Vision for Trade," *Dissent*, Winter 2017.

and to share battery technology with Chilean firms (whether private or public): US companies shouldn't use patents to monopolize manufacturing technologies, for example, and then sell batteries made with Chilean lithium back to Chileans at exorbitant prices. Government contracts, subsidies, and loans for green technology can also play a role in setting standards. A federal contract to provide lithium for electric buses, for example, could come with a requirement that supplies meet standards jointly negotiated with Chilean labor and Indigenous activists.

The United States has an important role to play, but it can't act alone. These trade and procurement policies could be part of agreements across countries where political parties have recently committed to a Green New Deal, including the United Kingdom's Labour Party, Spain's Socialist Party, and Canada's New Democratic Party. A "club" of countries pursuing Green New Deal–style legislation—ideally linking member states in the Global North and Global South—could facilitate this process. Members would pursue collective, binding policy goals based on shared principles of aggressive decarbonization and egalitarian social policy—a more concrete approach than previous attempts at global cooperation. Supply chain justice would make an excellent first challenge for such transnational cooperation to tackle.

For instance, since there are limits to how many renewable energy inputs—like lithium, cobalt, copper, and so on—we can safely mine, reining in US demand makes more of those resources available for other countries to use.

American efficiency would be ethical—and a key practical step to help other countries decarbonize.

None of this will be easy to achieve. Restrictions on mining would elicit fierce backlash from big companies and their allies in resource-intensive countries, often including local police forces and private security guards. Democratic controls on trade would likewise spur backlash from the multinational corporations, many based in the United States, that benefit from minimal regulation. And governments, no matter how progressive, won't succeed in reshaping the global economic order without significant pressure from mobilized constituents. Transforming renewable energy supply chains will require social organization, transnational alliances, and disruptive capacity.

Where are the openings for grassroots leverage in the globally interconnected energy system? Right now, that system is dominated by fossil fuels—and protest against fossil fuel infrastructure is increasingly connecting local and global action. The politics around this infrastructure are different from those around renewable energy. But they show that community and worker power is the supply-side complement to demand-side interventions to reduce energy consumption.

The fracking boom and the repeal of the ban on oil exports has made the United States a major fossil fuel exporter. We need to keep oil, coal, and gas in the ground, which means that every local battle against a liquified natural gas (LNG) plant, a pipeline, or a fracking project is part of the fight for a safer climate. From the Pacific Northwest to the Gulf Coast, carbon-spewing and explosive LNG export terminals are disproportionately located in poor neighborhoods and communities of color. These struggles against environmental injustice are also fights against the global fossil fuel sector. And they're making an impact: In a recent victory for the coalition against the Jordan Cove LNG facility in Oregon, the state's Department of Energy Quality denied the project's water permit.[14]

Protestors have also put their bodies in front of bulldozers and guard dogs to stop oil and gas pipelines. From April 2016 to February 2017, thousands gathered at the confluence of the Missouri and Cannonball Rivers in the Standing Rock Sioux Indian Reservation to prevent the construction of the Dakota Access Pipeline, which threatened the reservation's water supply.

Water Protectors faced brutal state repression, including mass arrests, water cannons, and attack dogs. But despite the violence, they drew on hundreds of years of Oceti Sakowin resistance to build, in Nick Estes's words, "an infrastructure of Indigenous resistance and caretaking" of each other and of the land.[15] At its height, as many as 15,000

---

14   Ted Sickenger, "Oregon DEQ Denies Jordan Cove LNG Water Quality Permit," *Oregonian*, May 6, 2019.

15   Nick Estes, *Our History Is the Future: Standing Rock versus the Dakota Access Pipeline and the Long Tradition of Indigenous Resistance* (Verso 2019), p. 58.

were present, comprising Water Protectors from almost 400 Indigenous nations, as well as many non-Indigenous allies—including Alexandria Ocasio-Cortez, who credited the experience with inspiring her to go into politics.[16]

As noted, we'll need some minerals from the earth to pull off an energy transition. But when it comes to similar actions at mines linked to renewable energy, community and labor resistance could slow the rate of environmentally damaging extraction, buying time to develop more environmentally sensitive technology and research into recycling and reusing lithium batteries. Lessons from the work of Water Protectors and the ongoing struggles in the Atacama Desert will be vital.[17] Supply and demand side restrictions can operate in tandem: When communities set higher labor and environmental standards around extraction, the price goes up, which incentivizes rich countries to build public buses instead of private cars. And when procurement and investment are guided by a democratic state rather than private capital, cutting prices at all costs is no longer the imperative.

The organization of the interlinked lithium mining, battery, and electric vehicle sectors also presents opportunities for strategic disruption. Lithium mining is a relatively oligopolistic market: a few firms control most projects.

16 Nick Bowlin, "Ocasio-Cortez's Unlikely Path to Becoming Green Hero," eenews.com, December 5, 2018.
17 Dave Sherwood, "In Chilean Desert, Global Thirst for Lithium Is Fueling a 'Water War,'" Reuters, August 29, 2018.

That concentration of ownership means that protests or strikes at any given mine have greater impact. Meanwhile, electric vehicle manufacturers are entering into direct agreements with lithium companies to ensure access to lithium supplies—which means that supply concerns have forced firms into vertical integration. While such agreements assure resource flows, they also create new risks. If the communities and workers at the mines where VW or BMW source their lithium decided to protest or strike, their actions would quickly leapfrog to the electric vehicle factory floor. The effect of that disruption could telescope vast networks and reverse the usual vectors of power. Maybe they would get support from long-distance comrades, like in 1978, when Oakland's International Longshore and Warehouse Union Local 10 refused to load ships transporting bombs to Pinochet's brutal regime in Chile, or from workers currently organizing in Tesla factories.

This kind of organizing is the grassroots counterpart to the trade policies discussed above. Imagine if workers in electric bus factories and urban transit authorities, in solidarity with Water Protectors and workers in lithium mines in Chile and the United States, pushed for corporate accountability, and threatened labor strikes and community direct actions if fleets of buses aren't produced in union-made supply chains—or if they threaten vulnerable watersheds, whether in the Atacama Desert or Death Valley.

As we've argued, addressing the planetary dimensions of climate change will require tackling the global dimensions of contemporary capitalism. We do that by building solidarity across borders, leveraging the choke points of the global economy in alliance with leftists holding state power. An effective Green New Deal is an internationalist one.

CONCLUSION: FREEDOM TO LIVE

Picture workers around the country, their arms and legs crisscrossed by thin red scrapes and studded with mosquito bites, planting trees in degraded forests alongside seed-dropping drones buzzing above; restoring the wetlands on delicate coasts; building green infrastructure by roadways and streams to help cities absorb floodwaters and keep their sewage systems clean. As they work, they see turbine blades turning in the wind and photovoltaic cells glinting in the sunlight.

Picture intercity travel that's carbon-free, clean, quiet, and fast. Amtrak's familiar routes run more often and cost less. Electric buses speed through dedicated highway lanes, while public electric minivans shuttle people around towns and suburbs. All over the country, unionized workers are laying tracks for efficient new trains. It's easy, affordable, and comfortable to go from Los Angeles to

San Francisco for a sister's birthday, from Dallas to Austin for a museum opening, from Milwaukee to Madison for a basketball tournament.

Picture diverse crowds roaming parks in any city or lounging beachside by lakes and oceans. There are tuition-free college students toting flasks, carrots, and edibles. There are parents talking to their kids about art class and pre-k reading circles. Teens and grownups play lively pickup games on new soccer fields and volleyball in the sand. See two lovers in Cleveland coming home from a Friday afternoon date picking berries in the countryside, drowsy from the bus ride back into town. They have Fridays off because their guaranteed jobs—one in the natural history museum, the other at the new municipal compost center—pay a good wage for a four-day week. When they get home, they stroll into the lush courtyard of a stylish new public housing complex.

Not every form of carbon-free, communal luxury that a radical Green New Deal promises is just around the corner. Yet the visions above could all be unfolding by the mid-2020s. They're consistent with rapid decarbonization, safeguards against extreme weather, and a long-term shift from the hyperprivatized consumption of things to the collective enjoyment of public services, pleasures, and time—and they're achievable in the short term.

We should keep these visions of a possible near-future in mind as we tackle the devilish details of decarbonizing. For decades, climate politics revolved around abstract plans that named targets like "80 by 50"—meaning 80 percent decarbonization by 2050. Such slogans were meaningless to those not in the know, and their long timelines were a gift to procrastinating politicians. By 2050, it'd be someone else's problem.

By contrast, we think fighting for a new world starts with imagining it viscerally. People mobilize around concrete projects that appeal to their desires and values. The climate fight will be a long one—but its projects need to bear fruit soon if they're to rouse the people fighting for change and energize them to keep pushing for more. Within a virtuous cycle of mobilization, each victory opens up new vistas of bigger dreams and bolder demands—and even campaigns that don't achieve all their goals can build power and raise expectations. The strategic corollary is that clear goals require clear opponents. As we've argued, "we" are not all responsible for the climate crisis in the same way—and we are not "all in it together." The broader our popular coalitions and the more contemptible our enemies—fossil fuel executives, craven politicians, private utilities, the landlord class—the stronger our movements. There is no middle ground on a warming planet.

"All Out," not "All or Nothing"

The age of climate gradualism is over. If we act too slowly, it will just be a matter of years before concatenating crises turn into an unimaginable nightmare. To stop that from happening, we need to go all out. But that's not the same as believing that every single fight, every single policy contest, every single election is "all or nothing." We fight for wind or solar, but will we give up and go home if the Department of the Interior approves more federal land for fracking? Will we give up if California's next governor is a climate moderate; if the Supreme Court shoots down a no-carbon, national public housing mandate; if we miss a net zero target by two years—or ten? Of course not.

Organizing has a reputation for being slow and steady—but history shows that it can accelerate fast. By that we don't just mean the New Deal. We can see momentum building today in the progressive forces that will be the backbone of the radical Green New Deal. As the labor organizer and author Jane McAlevey argues, the big victories of recent teachers' strikes in Chicago, West Virginia, and Los Angeles were the result of organizing that "transformed moribund, do-nothing organizations into unions capable of leading and winning all-out fights in which the opponents were strong and the odds were stiff."[1] McAlevey argues persuasively that smart, dedicated organizers can pull off this kind of turn-around in one to two years. The appetite for change is

1 Jane McAlevey, "Organizing to Win a Green New Deal," *Jacobin*, March 26, 2019, jacobinmag.com.

there—it's only the political infrastructure and concrete target that's missing.

In our approach to a Green New Deal strategy, we embrace McAlevey's call for 100 percent all-out strikes: shutting down business as usual to make a new order possible. Going "all out" means organizing the biggest group of people possible, getting them ready to fight, and then building power, win-by-win. You don't go on strike with a bare majority of workers with lukewarm support: if you do, you'll get crushed. Instead, you methodically build strength through increasingly challenging "structure tests"—first petition drives, then public rallies—and when the time comes to strike, you aim to get every worker to commit to going out for as long as it takes. Even almost-perfectly executed strikes still lose sometimes. But you don't give up the hospital campaign in St. Louis just because you lost in Minneapolis. You double down in St. Louis, then bring your victorious organizers back to Minneapolis to help them win on the second try. In the context of a disciplined campaign, even losses and setbacks develop organizers' skills, build relationships, test strategies, and set up the next round. Each win in these local brawls, meanwhile, fortifies organizing elsewhere. From striking teachers to Sunrise Movement sit-ins, there's far more momentum and possibility on the ground in the United States right now than you'd know from watching MSNBC.

We can't forget this—because even in the best-case scenario, with a radical Green New Deal pushed through amid financial and climate crises, there will be contention at every level of government and in every corner of the economy. There will be setbacks. That's premise, not punchline. If we didn't provoke retaliation from elites, we wouldn't be threatening their power. The more serious a climate program we have, the more opposition it will face. In fact, the greater the pushback, the more we know we're on the right track.

Then there's the grumbling from the fatalists: as climate change worsens, the merchants of doom will increasingly tell us it's too late, too much, and too hard. Our response to pessimism isn't a Pollyannaish optimism, but a commitment to collective action despite uncertainty. After all, things can always get worse. So part of today's "war of position" (to borrow a phrase from the Italian Marxist and social theorist Antonio Gramsci) is a trench war to hold off every extra tenth of a degree of warming. Each tiny tick upward in global temperatures translates to tens of thousands of lives lost, and will make the task of building a good world for all that much harder. The less carbon we emit, the fewer people die. The more public power we put toward winning clean energy, and decent housing, and green infrastructure, the more livable the future is for more people.

Virtuous Circles

Political change is uneven and multifaceted. There are long slogs of workaday organizing, sudden bursts of acceleration when opportunities appear, slow grinds of governance, defeats that send us back to the drawing board, and moments of rupture when everything is up for grabs. But even during the slowest and most painful stretches, two crucial things are happening: we're saving lives and buying time with every carbon reduction, while preparing for an opening for dramatic change that could come at any moment, at one of those rare times when sharp, structural change is possible in the heat of the crisis. The climate movement can only win its existential battles against fossil capital and other elites with numbers and organization—strengths built over time strike by strike, election by election, meeting by meeting, potluck by potluck.

When it comes to the Green New Deal, that means each fight should bring more people on board for the next one, in a virtuous cycle that broadens its social and political base and wins material improvements that lay the foundations for further victories. In each chapter of this book, we've shown how this might happen in different political-economic arenas.

Cutting carbon emissions quickly means doing away with their biggest source: the fossil fuel industry and its enablers. We can't avoid a confrontation. That means we need to directly take on the fossil fuel companies and private utilities whose business models rest on making the planet uninhabitable. It means going after them in specific cases when their culpability is unmistakable, as when the negligence of private utilities causes people to die horrifically in disasters like the Camp Fire, and relentlessly driving home the fossil fuel industry's responsibility for planetary destruction. It means feeding righteous Left-populist rage about the havoc that corporations and the wealthy have wreaked on our lives, and letting executives in other industries know we're coming for them next.

To bring labor on board, we need to cleave extractive sector workers away from their exploitative bosses. But the labor base for a Green New Deal must be much broader than the traditional energy sector. We need a just transition for labor that can win immediate benefits for the vast majority of workers. A federal job guarantee and revitalized collective bargaining rights will strengthen workers' position in the fight for better wages and working conditions, making it possible to demand and win more. A more expansive conception of green jobs centering carbon-free care work would bring social reproduction workers and their unions (many of which have been at the forefront of support for the Green New Deal) into the fight, while also delivering benefits to the general public. And labor organizing can stoke organizing in communities beyond the workplace, winning victories for workers and the people around them.

When it comes to the energy transition, a virtuous cycle means transforming the built environment to slash energy demand in ways that make life easier, more affordable, and more pleasant. Building out carbon-free public housing and expanding public transportation would connect the Green New Deal to working class struggles for affordable homes, effective transit, and desegregated communities. Projects to construct landscapes of public leisure, from urban swimming pools to rural biking trails, would improve the quality of life in cities, towns, suburbs, and reservations, and change the meaning of abundance. This is decarbonization as a vision not of deprivation but of open space and public luxury—a more pleasant world for all with time to enjoy it, starting now.

Any climate program worth its salt has to take the rest of the world seriously, and so does any Left. We see the supply chains of the Green New Deal as a crucial site for weaving international solidarity and constructing new mechanisms for the global cooperation that climate action requires. The renewable energy transition can't come at the cost of ecosystems and communities in other parts of the world. We see the growing trade in resources like lithium as an opportunity to push back on the neoliberal model of globalization and build something else in its place. Workers and communities are more powerful when they ally across borders—so we envision solidarity campaigns to hold corporations accountable at the sites of mineral extraction, and push for a US trade policy that puts environmental and labor standards above corporate profits. In turn, this would help an American Green New Deal prompt faster decarbonization everywhere.

These aren't the only battles to come. Health, education, transit, agriculture, trade, public investment, reproductive justice, immigration: All of these familiar issues will be transformed by climate chaos. Each is a site of contestation over the twenty-first century's defining questions: Can we prevent runaway climate breakdown? And who gets to live, and live well, in our warming world?

Stop Eco-apartheid

This book maps out the more equal and democratic world we believe we can build instead of the one we fear will come about otherwise. There are plenty of climate apocalypse scenarios out there already. But in closing, it's worth remembering what's at stake. We're calling for an all-out charge toward the world we've laid out here not just because it'd be nice to live in—though it would!—but because the alternative is so much worse. And when the climate is changing, there's no standing still.

Another four years of the Trump administration is an obvious nightmare. It will mean losing precious time to decarbonize, but it will also fuel a vicious circle: concentration camps and racial violence; expanded drilling and a more powerful fossil fuel industry; the further dismantling of labor rights and weakened unions. But there are many paths to a hellish earth, and another one leads right down the center of the political aisle.

It's clear that the political establishment is collapsing both in the United States and beyond. Clinging to it makes it possible for reactionaries like Trump to gain more ground the world over and brings climate catastrophe closer. The fundamental issue is this: As the center shrinks and the time for decarbonization tightens, milquetoast climate action on the margins will satisfy hardly anyone. If centrist Democrats spurn the insurgent Left and instead see centrist Republicans as their most reliable allies, they'll pull the planet out of the frying pan—and into the fire. Stopping a surging Right from a revitalized and resolute Left will be hard enough. Stopping it from a mushy center will be impossible.

We've shown how past efforts at climate bipartisanship have failed. Now, bipartisanship means compromising with a resolutely xenophobic Right. Imagine establishment Democrats and Republicans agreeing to an infrastructure deal that trades major investments in solar panels for a border wall and sharp restrictions on migrants from Central America fleeing climate change, agricultural sector collapse, and dirty wars—all fueled by US policy, needless to say. Each year, more people would die in the intensifying desert heat or languish in ICE detention centers. Across the Atlantic, as heat waves sweep Europe, Marine Le Pen's National Front Party in France might join forces with Italy's League and Denmark's increasingly xenophobic Social Democrats, to entrench crumbling European welfare states behind a hardened Frontex wall of violence, which already kills thousands of climate refugees attempting to cross the Mediterranean from an African continent suffering worsening droughts.

This is the eco-apartheid nightmare we're desperate to prevent—and it's frighteningly close. We know the proponents of more moderate climate action don't want it to happen either. Most progressives concerned about climate change are repulsed by right-wing nationalism. But we don't think the measures moderates have offered can prevent it. In fact, Democrats don't even have to make deals with the Right to bring this future closer. By offering more of the same to a country desperate for change, Democrats will clear the way for the racist Right to keep consolidating its power. We've already explained why we think nudges like tax incentives are inadequate on policy grounds. But even if they weren't, we don't see campaign pledges for a market-driven energy transition winning elections against a Right tapping into long-simmering frustration and rage, while tens of millions of demoralized voters stay home. It doesn't matter how efficient a carbon tax is if it can't win popular support. The move from Barack Obama to Donald Trump in the United States is a hint of what we can expect if we go further down that road.

Elites take the rise of far-Right populism as confirmation that the irrational and ill-informed masses are incapable of addressing climate change and perhaps incapable of governing themselves at all. But we're not going to blame democracy for the mess capitalism has made. We see the people not as an obstacle to climate action, but as the engine of a just transition. As we've argued here, a Left populism that mobilizes a genuinely multiracial working class is an essential step in the path to creating a more equal and just society—one that can weather climate change and prevent its most catastrophic effects. That kind of politics draws a sharp line between the masses of excluded and exploited who are likely to suffer the most, and the rich and powerful who benefit from the status quo. A Left populist agenda will have its setbacks, but it also has a giant upside—people to keep fighting with and for in the long run. For better and for worse, our choice now is between eco-socialism or eco-apartheid. So instead of the third-way environmentalism of the 1980s—neither Left nor Right but forward; not red but green—we need to pose a simple question: Which side are you on?

Toward freedom

For the Right, the Green New Deal represents the eco-totalitarian takeover. As Sebastian Gorka, a former deputy advisor to President Trump, told the Conservative Political Action Conference, "They want to take your pickup truck, they want to rebuild your home, they want to take away your hamburgers. This is what Stalin dreamt about but never achieved."[2] The Trump administration's Department of Energy has meanwhile sought to rebrand natural gas as "freedom gas."[3]

But as historian Kim Phillips-Fein reminds us, manufactured panic about looming totalitarianism is a trick out of an old playbook: "We've seen pretty much this same furor over imperiled liberty and hovering tyranny in the concerted bid from some business leaders to stigmatize and delegitimize the original New Deal."[4] Too much, too fast, too soon: business leaders concern-trolled the debate about the New Deal to defuse the threat of public intervention. And when organized labor undertook the massive strikes that actually won the New Deal victories, liberals fretted that they were going too far.

If the Right used the language of freedom in failed efforts to prevent the New Deal era from being born, they also deployed it successfully to hasten its death. In his 1979 book *Free to Choose*, Milton Friedman observed that although

New Deal liberalism has crested, there is as yet no clear evidence whether the tide that succeeds it will be toward

2   Antonia Noori Farzan, "The Latest Right-wing Attack on Democrats: 'They Want to Take Away your Hamburgers,'" *Washington Post*, March 1, 2019.

3   John Bowden, "Trump Energy Officials Label Natural Gas 'Freedom Gas,'" *The Hill*, May 29, 2019. thehill.com.

4   Kim Phillips-Fein, "Fear and Loathing of the Green New Deal," *New Republic*, May 29, 2019.

greater freedom and limited government ... or toward an omnipotent monolithic government in the spirit of Marx and Mao.[5]

Friedman, like FDR, called for an economic Bill of Rights. But where FDR's made public commitments to universal economic well-being for the good of the general populace, Friedman suggested limiting the power of the government to tax and spend in the name of individual freedom.

The libertarian vision of freedom as your right as an individual to do whatever you want—so long as you can pay for it—is a recipe for disaster in the twenty-first century, when it's clearer than ever that our fates are bound up together. We now live on an earth scorched by Friedman's so-called freedoms. By contrast, the Left's vision of freedom has always meant something different than the capitalist's freedom to invest or the consumer's freedom to buy. And we think a big and bold enough Green New Deal can help us get truly free.

Formally, we look to a New Deal–era statement of principles: FDR's Four Freedoms, declared in 1941 as New Deal progress faltered and war in Europe loomed. But our vision of freedom is more in line with the principles of the Freedom Budget for All Americans—a riff on FDR's economic bill of rights that was developed by the Black

---

5 Milton Friedman and Rose Friedman, *Free to Choose: A Personal Statement* (Harcourt 1980), p. 284.

freedom struggle in the 1960s, challenging America's racist order two decades into the New Deal era.[6] Race was one of the New Deal's great failings: Northern liberals supportive of FDR let the "southern cage" of white supremacist Democrats impose racial exclusions on supposedly universalist New Deal programs, with the result of hardening Jim Crow.[7]

But bargain with the devil and the devil wins. As the great sociologist W.E.B. Du Bois observed, when white progressives sell out people of color, they inflict a mortal wound on the entire working class and ultimately, on their own stated projects. Against the racist compromises of centrism, Du Bois drew on the brief, radical program of Black Reconstruction to counterpose "abolition democracy": a political economic vision of taking from the few to empower the many, by building on Black radicalisms rather than betraying them. He argued that true empowerment came when working people, starting with emancipated Black Americans, seized equal power over the economy.[8]

The Freedom Budget for All Americans followed in the tradition of abolition democracy. It called for full

---

6   A. Philip Randolph and Bayard Rustin, "A 'Freedom Budget' for All Americans: A Summary," A. Philip Randolph Institute, January 1967, prrac.org/pdf/FreedomBudget.pdf.

7   Ira Katznelson, *Fear Itself: The New Deal and the Origins of Our Time* (Liveright 2013).

8   W.E.B. Du Bois, *Black Reconstruction in America* (Harcourt Brace, 1935).

employment and a guaranteed adequate income; for decent housing and medical care; for improvements to transportation and the end of air and water pollution. As the legendary organizer Bayard Rustin put it, the civil rights movement was "fighting for total freedom ... for every economic, political, and social right that is presently denied."[9] Today, scholar-activists like Ruth Wilson Gilmore are carrying that torch, arguing that abolition democracy entails rigorous, rooted organizing to replace the prison-industrial complex with a form of economic development that protects ecosystems, abolishes racism, and empowers workers.[10] A Green New Deal won't just make people freer by making them less unequal—it will give them the ability to build their own lives within our common world. To that end, we suggest a vision of five freedoms that can guide us into an uncertain future.

Freedom from Fear

FDR called for freedom from fear of military conflict. We're still working on disarmament—we could start with the US Army, the world's biggest consumer of oil and a purveyor of fear worldwide. But we must transform our built environment to grant us freedom from fear of the

---

9   Bayard Rustin, "The Meaning of Birmingham," *Liberation*, June 1963, crmvet.org.

10   "Making Abolition Geography in California's Central Valley: An Interview with Ruth Wilson Gilmore," *Funambulist Magazine*, January– February 2019.

physical changes that already locked-in global warming will bring: fire and hurricanes, extreme temperatures, sea level rise and storm surges—and freedom from the fear that those dangers will grow exponentially worse. It also means abolishing the social disasters a volatile planet could exacerbate. We need freedom from food scarcity and water shortages; freedom from racist, colonial, and sexual violence; and freedom from militarized borders. Freedom from fear means guaranteed jobs and homes so that we can survive every storm, every relocation, and every reorganization of industry.

Freedom from Toil

We can't escape work altogether, and there's a lot of work we need to do, immediately and in the long term. But work doesn't need to rule our lives. The great nineteenth-century English socialist William Morris made a distinction between useful work and useless toil: We need the former but should work to free ourselves from the latter. We can escape the crushing toll of working long hours for low wages to make something that someone else owns. At present, there's a lot of work that's worse than useless—work that's harmful to the people doing it and to the world in which we live. But even useful work should be distributed more widely so that we can all do less of it—and spend more time enjoying its fruits.

Freedom from Domination

We must continue to pursue freedom not only from toil, but from the despotism of the boss; freedom from a viciously enforced racial order and the intimate power of patriarchy. Domination also names our helplessness in the face of global capitalism. Liberals say the market gives us freedom to choose. But under capitalism, the market is master, determining what we can do and who we can be. Every hour of every day, the compulsion of the market stamps its will on every aspect of our lives. The Left has long sought to end the arbitrary power of the few over the many. Now, the outrageous power of the few threatens billions with ruin. We need to know it's possible to change our own fate, to be able to imagine the end of capitalism more easily than the end of the world. We need to chase old freedom dreams to build a better future. But we must also let go of old dreams of achieving freedom by recklessly dominating nature to serve human ends. Those dreams have turned into nightmares. We need to live on this earth with other people and other species. With innovation, equality, and wisdom, we can all have freedom within the necessity of planetary limits.

Freedom to Move

We live on a beautiful planet that belongs to everyone— we should all be free to move around it. Freedom to move is particularly crucial for those whose homes are being rendered unlivable by rising temperatures and seas. To cope with inevitable climate displacements, we need solidarity without fences or walls. The freedom to move means the freedom to pack up and live in another city, region, or country—but also the freedom to stay put in the face of capital's relentless uprooting, to stay rooted in the communities and places that matter to us instead of being forced to migrate to survive. Whether we stay in place or relocate, we should be free to travel to enjoy our vibrant world's wonders. Maybe not as quickly as we do now—we can't all fly everywhere at the drop of a hat. But it's the reckless waste of the affluent that must end, not the ordinary person's occasional pleasure in discovering a new world. We need to move around in our ordinary lives, too—and for that we need free, and carbon-free, public transit to get around day-to-day without intensifying the carbon crisis.

Freedom to Live

There is enough on our Earth for people everywhere to have what they need to live well. Reusing, recycling, and—most important—redistributing our abundance will open new vistas. The freedom to live well includes freedom from want: plentiful access to the basics, like food, drink, shelter, health care, dental, education, music, art, and green spaces. People are also entitled to freedom to want: the freedom to enjoy life, to be creative, to produce and delight in communal luxuries, to soak up the public goods we create for everyone's pleasure, to love those we love, and to find new people to love, too. The freedom to live a good life means enjoying the wonders of knowledge, leisure, and adventure.

Enemies of climate action warn of gray totalitarianism even as the fossil industry commits crimes against humanity to maintain the privileges of a few. The point of a radical Green New Deal is to build the opposite: a colorful democracy for all, to live through sun and storm.

ACKNOWLEDGMENTS

This book was written as a collective endeavor, under the pressure of fast-evolving climate politics and accelerating signs of the climate emergency. We built on a foundation of knowledge and commitments enriched with new inquiries, unexpected findings, and still nascent possibilities. This orientation—experimental, collaborative, with an ear to the ever-shifting ground—is inspired by the radical promise of a Green New Deal.

Along the way, we've been helped—questioned, challenged, and edified—by an expansive community of colleagues and comrades. We're beyond grateful for the generosity of David Backer, Margaret Badding, Ramón Balcázar, Johanna Bozuwa, Neil Brenner, Gareth Dale, Daniel Denvir, Ethan Earle, Mark Engler, Billy Fleming, Liz Greenspan, Andy Horowitz, Sarah Jaffe, Jesse Jenkins, Sarah Knuth, Thomas Kruse, Mathew Lawrence, Lida

Maxwell, Dustin Mulvaney, Jedediah Purdy, Nicholas Pevzner, Nikil Saval, Quinn Slobodian, David Stein, Leah Stokes, Astra Taylor, Simon Torracinta, and Gabriel Winant. We're thrilled to have a foreword from Naomi Klein, who has done so much to advance the climate left. We're deeply appreciative that she took the time while finishing her own book on the Green New Deal. We've also learned enormously from all the contributors to our ongoing Green New Deal series at *Jacobin*, made possible by the editorial support of Shawn Gude and Micah Uetricht. Sections of this book contain revised text and ideas from some of the articles that we wrote in that series.

We're also appreciative of our institutional backers, who facilitated our research and writing in 2019. Kate thanks the Type Media Center; Alyssa thanks Yale University and the Brooklyn Institute for Social Research; Daniel thanks the University of Pennyslvania and the Institute for Advanced Study in Princeton, New Jersey; and Thea thanks Providence College and El Núcleo Milenio en Energía y Sociedad (NUMIES) in Chile.

Finally, we're tremendously thankful to Asher Dupuy-Spencer, Bhaskar Sunkara, and the entire Verso team for believing in this project and for their thoughtful guidance throughout the process.